G000277496

A BLONDE IN
THE BAZAAR

A glance at the heart's skirts saying . . . this is the place.
Emperor Jahangir, ruler of the Indian subcontinent 1605–27

For Derek, Rachel and Jonathan

A BLONDE IN
THE BAZAAR

JILL WORRALL

NEW
HOLLAND

First published in 2003 by New Holland Publishers (NZ) Ltd
Auckland • Sydney • London • Cape Town

218 Lake Road, Northcote, Auckland, New Zealand
14 Aquatic Drive, Frenchs Forest, NSW 2086, Australia
86–88 Edgware Road, London W2 2EA, United Kingdom
80 McKenzie Street, Cape Town 8001, South Africa

www.newhollandpublishers.com

Copyright © 2003 in text: Jill Worrall
Copyright © 2003 in photography:
  Author photograph: John Bisset
  Back cover photograph: Mujahid Ali Khan
  Inside photographs: Mujahid Ali Khan and Jill Worrall
Copyright © 2003 New Holland Publishers (NZ) Ltd

Publishing manager: Renée Lang
Cover design: Dexter Fry
Book design: Alison Dench
Editor: Anna Rogers

Worrall, Jill.
A blonde in the bazaar / Jill Worrall.
ISBN 1-86966-030-7
1. Worrall, Jill—Journeys—Pakistan. 2. Pakistan—Description and
travel. I. Title.
915.491045—dc 21

10 9 8 7 6 5 4 3 2 1

Colour reproduction by PICA Colour Separation, Singapore
Printed by McPherson's Printing Group, Australia

All rights reserved. No part of this publication may be reproduced,
stored in a retrieval system, or transmitted in any form or by any means,
electronic, mechanical, photocopying, recording or otherwise,
without the prior permission of the publishers and copyright holders.

contents

acknowledgements

I would never have been able to spend so much time being a blonde in the bazaars of Pakistan, and then writing about it, if it were not for the help and support of family, friends and colleagues, both in New Zealand and in Pakistan.

My thanks to Michael Meadowcroft, who introduced me to Pakistan. The fact that he has always loved the place, both the good and the bad, profoundly influenced my attitude to the country from the outset.

Thank you, too, to Pat and Murray Reedy of Greymouth, who took a gamble on my writing abilities and so generously allowed me to travel on one of their small group tours.

The Asia 2000 organisation in New Zealand also helped fund one of my most recent trips to Pakistan, and I want to acknowledge their support and that of my employers, *Timaru Herald* editor Dave Wood and general manager Barry Appleby,

acknowledgements

who have tolerated my absences and allowed me some flexibility to carry out my travels. And thank you to my long-suffering colleagues who were lumbered with extra shifts in my absences.

And to Renée Lang at New Holland Publishers, who has always had more faith in my ability to write a book than me! Her enthusiastic support has been wonderful, as has been the help from the rest of the team.

Before the manuscript even reached New Holland, Lindsay Mutch wore out several red pens editing the initial drafts. Thank you so much, my friend.

To the cast of, well, if not thousands, then at least dozens of people in Pakistan, who have made my travels not only possible but always magical: *Bahut bahut mehrebani*. Thank you to Tayyab and Sadaf, Umer, Innayat, Qudar Ali Shah, Ali Nazaar, Karim and Paree, Wafi and Fatima, Hunar, Roima, Naseema, Najma and Murad, Mohammed, Ali and all the other wonderful people who made me welcome.

And to Mujahid. Without him most of these journeys would not have been the truly memorable experience they were. Thank you for giving me my much-loved Pakistani extended family.

The words 'thank you' don't quite seem sufficient for my husband Derek. I could not have made any of these journeys without his love and support (and access to what's left in the joint account). And I could never have written about them without the confidence he gave me (and all the help with the damn computer).

Why look for another Moon, or another Sun
What I see will always be enough for me

author's note

This book is based on four journeys I have made to Pakistan over an 18-year period. Some of the chapters are the result of several visits to the same place so, to save readers from a temporal version of motion sickness, I have not attempted to write the book in chronological order. Instead it loosely follows a geographic progression from mountains to deserts to cities.

have a pakistani takeaway

It would have been the ultimate souvenir. 'You want to go home with a Pakistani baby boy?' He wasn't offering me a babe in arms, more a baby in the making, to put it delicately. And, of course, it would have been a boy. Pakistan may be a paid-up member of the nuclear arms club but the age-old belief linking virility and the production of boy babies lives on.

I declined this generous and enterprising offer. My long-suffering husband had only just begun coping with my weakness for bringing home hand-knotted carpets. A baby could be one import too many. And anyway, Pakistan was already in my blood. It seeped in there nearly 20 years ago. It only takes an insistent car horn, the twirl of a bright scarf, wood smoke at dusk and, with an immediate and painful tug at the heart, my mind takes me back there.

I'd never given Pakistan much thought until at the age of 16

I started talking to the new kid at school. He was tall, thin with daringly long hair for our very conservative college and spoke with a strange hybrid accent – New Zealand, American and something I just couldn't put my finger on. Michael was a Kiwi but he'd been born in Pakistan to New Zealand missionaries and he lived there until he was 16. To me, growing up in Christchurch, New Zealand, in a circle of family and friends who were all home-grown like me, this was a fascinating concept.

He'd spoken almost better Urdu (Pakistan's national language) than English until he was school age, the result of playing with the local kids who lived in his home town at Gujranwala in the Punjab. Then, when they were six and a half, he and his twin sister were sent to boarding school at Murree in the Himalayan foothills, about an hour's drive uphill from Pakistan's capital, Islamabad. This was a school predominantly for missionaries' children and when Michael attended most of the teachers, boarding staff and students were from the States. This explained the amalgam of sounds in his accent.

And now he was in Christchurch. There were no dudh wallahs biking along the road outside his house with their brass pots of fresh milk, no call to morning prayer from the mosque, no walk through the deodar pines of Murree every morning from the boys' hostel to the school perched on the edge of a hill with a view north to the hidden ramparts of the Karakoram Mountains.

Now, more than ever, I understand how hard the adjustment must have been. Michael was told it must be good to be home – but home wasn't the orderly streets of Christchurch, it was the chaos of a dusty Pakistani bazaar. A milkshake from the dairy wasn't the same as sitting in the back of a gloomy village tea shop drinking chai and eating crispy parathas glossy with oil. His parents had worked in Pakistan for over 20 years so his family home was full of reminders of the country. There were pottery and camel-skin lamps from Multan, embroidered cushion covers from the Punjab, inlaid wooden furniture from Lahore, mirrored hats from the Sind.

We married when I was 19 and four years later headed away on the great OE, planning to return to New Zealand in a year's time after spending several weeks in Pakistan on the way home. This was to be Michael's first visit there since his return to New Zealand and I couldn't wait to get there either: I'd become hooked on the place by proxy.

On a bone-freezing March morning in Herefordshire a letter arrived at the pub where we worked as bar staff. It was from Pakistan, from Murree Christian School, asking if, rather than just visiting the school for a few days, we'd like to come for three months to help out in the boarding hostel. The woman who looked after the senior girls was going on furlough and the organised replacement couldn't come.

Michael had just finished cleaning out the men's urinals and I'd been vacuuming the lounge bar which smelt of spilt beer and fusty cigarette smoke. There was no contest.

So, in the midst of a spectacular monsoonal deluge, we flew into Islamabad in August 1984. The Russians had invaded Afghanistan, sending millions of refugees flooding into Pakistan and somewhere, it was discovered later, a man named Osama was helping to co-ordinate the Afghan resistance. A few weeks later India's prime minister, Indira Gandhi, was assassinated, putting Pakistan on high alert as India was initially convinced that a Pakistani was responsible. (It turned out to be a Sikh.) An inhabitant of a small, insignificant nation at the bottom of the world, I was now in the middle of the action.

I'd never set foot in Asia before and I was bombarded with so many strange images, sounds, smells and sensations that my system shut down for days. I had culture shock. And just when I'd begun to feel at home we'd visit a Pakistani city where the contrasts were even more dramatic and vivid and it would start all over again. I developed cataclysmic stomach troubles, reeled at the beggars, craved chocolate and wanted to scream when everyone kept staring. And fell completely in love with the place.

The following years brought two children, a new job and then divorce and remarriage. But always at the back of my mind was the plan to go back one day. Ours had been a working holiday and there was so much of Pakistan I still wanted, still needed, to see. We hadn't been able to go up the Khyber Pass because it was alive with freedom fighters leaving the relatively safe haven of Peshawar to cross the mountains to kill Russians; there was much talk of the new Karakoram highway that linked Pakistan with China, one of the highest roads in the world, but it wasn't yet fully open to foreigners; I'd driven past the ruins of Taxila four times but had never been able to stop to see the place where Alexander the Great is believed to have halted and consulted the Buddhist scholars.

There was no money to travel but any travel brochure about companies running tours to Pakistan was squirrelled away just in case. Then, in 1999, a strange coincidence: the day I returned from collecting a travel writing award, a brochure arrived from Pat and Murray Reedy on New Zealand's West Coast. They ran small group tours to Pakistan and their pamphlet was full of photos of improbably rugged mountains, terraced hillsides pink with blossom and graceful Moghul architecture.

Would they take a travel writer, who now had at least a little credibility, on a tour at a cut price in return for some articles? They would. For the cost of my airfares I was going back to Pakistan, a three-week tour with a small group of women, not only sightseeing from Karachi in the south to Hunza in the north, but also meeting women's groups and development agencies, and visiting schools, hospitals and co-operatives.

During this tour I met the men and their families who ran the Pakistan-based tour company Karavan Leaders. I now have an ever-growing extended family of Pakistanis and with their help have been fulfilling long-held ambitions to explore the country in depth. And the more I travel in Pakistan the more I want to stay; every time I leave I take a little longer to come home.

when you've got to go

'Please lift up your dress,' the young Thai woman in Bangkok airport says as she runs the hand-held metal detector over me. It lets out a series of indignant beeps as it reaches my waist.

Behind me more than 100 people are lined up suffering the long wait with varying degrees of patience: they will enjoy this entertainment. As I'm wearing the traditional Pakistani outfit of long tunic top (a kameez) and loose-fitting trousers (shalwar), this means reaching below my knees to lift up the hem of the kameez, thus exposing the capacious gathered top of the trousers. This is not the done thing in Pakistan and I'm not thrilled at having to do it here either.

The official sees my money belt. 'Please take it off – I have to look inside it.'

'Can't you just look inside it while it's still on me?' I suggest, not wanting to have to rearrange my clothing any further in front of a now captivated audience. So while she rummages through the belt, which must have looked like some weird kind of open-air surgery to those behind me, I have time for my first attack of nerves about this final stage of a journey to Pakistan that has already suffered two false starts.

After the catastrophic events of September 11 2001, Pakistan was right next to the epicentre of some of the fallout. As the world turned its attention to neighbouring Afghanistan, Pakistan, too, became a permanent fixture in the 'don't go' category of travel advisories issued by most Western governments. International airlines cancelled flights and the country's tourist industry all but vanished overnight.

Then as a few visitors began to trickle back, disaster struck again. Pakistan and India plunged into their latest crisis over the festering problem of Kashmir (the predominantly Muslim state that is mostly governed by India but which every man and his water buffalo in Pakistan believe should be part of their nation). Millions of troops were massed on both sides of the border, new lines of defence were dug and there was talk around the world of nuclear war. Although I was convinced it would not come to this, I knew my planned trip to Pakistan would have to be postponed as too many people at home would suffer sleepless nights if I went.

The crisis cooled from boiling point to the usual simmer and I began to reorganise my trip. Then the country was dealt another series of body blows. Eleven French engineers (and three Pakistanis) were killed in a bomb explosion in Karachi (sending our cricket team, who'd been staying in the hotel across the road, fleeing home); six people were killed in a gun battle at Murree Christian School, which was on my itinerary; five

Pakistanis, including four nurses, were killed at the Taxila Christian Hospital; and five people had been shot dead at a church in Islamabad.

Again, I didn't think that as a lone tourist travelling with Pakistanis I would be a target for a lunatic fringe of fanatics. But, while Westerners were being encouraged to catch the next flight home I could not convince my family that I'd be okay heading in the opposite direction. I postponed again.

Throughout these events I was in contact with my friends in the travel industry in Lahore. As I watched post-Afghanistan invasion pictures of rioting and protests in Pakistani cities I rang my closest friend at Karavan Leaders to see if he was all right. I had visions of all my Pakistani nearest and dearest holed up in the office fearing for their lives.

'Yes, of course, we're all right,' Mujahid said, sounding surprised I'd rung.

'But it sounds awful – I'm watching it on CNN now.'

The words CNN brought a snort of derision from Mujahid. Many Pakistanis were angry about what they regarded as an 'anti-Muslim' spin that CNN and other news networks had put on George W. Bush's 'war against terror'.

'We're fine. Look at it this way – you're a film crew sitting in the Pearl Continental [one of Lahore's top hotels] and it's costing your bosses thousands of dollars a day. So, you have to find something to do. You go out into the bazaar and there's me buying some socks [Mujahid loses socks in direct proportion to the way he attracts women] or round the corner there's two idiots who draw an American flag on a piece of cardboard and set fire to it. What are you going to film?'

When the two countries began digging in along the border

I rang again, and this time got Umer, the operations manager in the Lahore office. It was about a 45-minute drive from the border.

'I thought you might all have gone to the hills,' I said.

'Why?' he replied, mystified.

'Just the possibility that you're going to be nuked with a missile.'

'Oh that! We're thinking like this: we're so close to the border they won't hit us because it will affect people in India. The missiles will go right over our heads.' He was laughing. No one in Pakistan believed there was going to be a war, nuclear or otherwise.

After that I stopped ringing every time there was a new calamity. It was an expensive way to provide some amusement for everyone during their all too quiet days in the office. But, in the face of a downturn that would have defeated many businessmen, they were somehow staying optimistic. Of course, they had little choice and plenty of practice at weathering political upheaval.

'You're in the news almost every day. You must hate all this negative publicity,' I said.

'No, no,' said Mujahid. 'At least now everyone knows where we are.'

I decided it was time to return to Pakistan.

But the almost obsessive security in Bangkok brings home to me that, although I have few doubts about my safety, others are not convinced. I've ignored New Zealand government advice that travel to Pakistan should be avoided. I could get no travel insurance and some of my family and friends expect to see me next starring on the news as an al-Qaeda hostage, or worse.

I'm on the final stretch now – only a few minutes' wait at the departure lounge and I'll be on the plane. I know once I get to Lahore I'll feel fine but like just about every airline passenger I can't shake from my mind the spectre of those towers of flames, smoke and death. I make the long walk down the ramp to the rows of plastic seats, knowing that as one of the few Western woman on the flight I'll be well scrutinised by those who have already checked in. But I'm distracted by another new addition to the security arrangements: the presence of half a dozen more security staff, three wearing latex gloves, who are waiting before the check-in counter. Gloves? Surely not . . .

I'm almost relieved to find they are merely making a minute check of our hand luggage, which has already been scanned once. Almost relieved because inside my backpack is a 3-litre cask of red wine. Taking this into a Muslim nation where there is an official ban on alcohol might give me the kind of reception committee I could do without.

I'd been asked to bring the wine because I've been invited to a wedding in Hunza in the mountains of northern Pakistan where many of the inhabitants blithely disregard both government and religious edicts on drinking. I'd not be bothered by Pakistani customs people, my friends said, because I was a Westerner. And, what's more, the staff on the X-ray machines didn't know about cask wine. The Thais certainly aren't interested in the wine. They are looking for explosives and weapons. Yet another body search follows. By now I am a bundle of nerves. Am I really being irresponsible travelling to a country that inspires such measures?

I step off the plane at Lahore and am met by the warm humid air of a November night. The X-ray machine drinks in the wine, swills it around and spits it out. I am free to go.

Hundreds of people, almost all of them men, are standing outside the arrivals hall, peering into the customs area. I remember the first time I'd walked this gauntlet in Islamabad and how overwhelmed I'd been. I'm used to it now and what's more I have friends to find in the crush. And there they are – Mujahid, Tayyab and Shahjee – waving and smiling. The world might have changed irreparably since I last walked through these doors but the Pakistani welcome has not.

There's Mujahid, a stocky man from the mountains, with black curly hair, a moustache and closely trimmed goatee beard. And what he complacently describes, with some justification, as killer eyes. He's holding a bouquet of red roses for me. Shahjee is also from the mountains. A man who smiles easily, he has a finely sculpted face, weather-beaten from a lifetime of high alpine climbing and trekking; he gives me an affectionate clip around the head. Tayyab, a man of the plains, a Punjabi, has a luxuriant moustache. He is a thinker, a philosopher who is drawn to the Sufi tradition of mystical Islam. They are part of the Karavan Leaders team, the tour company that now has almost no tourists to look after. The fruits of years of painstaking marketing and weeks, even months, away from their families guiding tourists have withered away because of events over which they had no control.

Before September 11, Pakistanis in the tourist industry sometimes described their country as Asia's best kept secret. And after living there, and travelling from Karachi to high in the Karakoram, I agreed with them. India had tended to grab all the kudos for being the essence of the exotic East, Nepal was known as the place to go for mountains, and thousands of overland travellers from the 1960s and 1970s remembered Pakistan as the country you passed through going to and from the much trendier Afghanistan. Meanwhile, the few thousand tourists who came to Pakistan each year learnt what generations of Pakistanis already knew – that their country had some of the most glorious mountain scenery on earth and evidence of thousands of years of history was often literally strewn on the ground. And it was populated by people for whom hospitality to visitors was an intrinsic part of life.

Unfortunately, Pakistan had been dogged by a bad press even before September 11. Admittedly it was difficult to put a positive spin on wars with India and military coups, but Pakistan never seemed to get a break. If there was a story in the international press about Pakistan that was not about border clashes with India over Kashmir, then internal conflicts were in the headlines. Television footage on Pakistan seemed limited to shots of policemen armed to the teeth hurtling along highways in open trucks and wild-looking tribesmen in turbans glaring at the camera.

And now the world's perceptions had become further confused. Pakistan is a Muslim country (about 97 per cent of Pakistanis are Muslims) so many foreigners believed that the whole population had been mobilised as mujahideen against the evil West, or were at least hostile to outsiders. Islam is badly misunderstood in the West and ignorance breeds fear. For Westerners, the words Muslim and fundamentalism have become inextricably linked and the word terrorist is thrown in for good measure.

I've sat in a house 2500 metres up in the Karakorams that is packed with Muslims all giving thanks to Allah for their food;

watched an elderly man smile serenely at me then eat a single date as he breaks the Ramazan fast after more than 12 hours without food or drink, his lips moving silently in prayer; I've stood on a rooftop and heard the muezzin singing, telling the faithful to come to prayer, come to security; every day there I lose count of the times I say 'Asalaam aleikum' – the peace upon you, say goodbye with the words 'Khuda hafiz' – God (be your) protector. These people have as much connection with terrorism as your average Anglican vicar has with the Holocaust.

You can't live or travel in Pakistan and not be aware of the way Islam reaches into every part of people's lives. The word Islam means peace that comes from absolute surrender to Allah (God). Allah's will for mankind is written in the Koran, which Muslims try to follow. The essential ingredients of Islam, as practised by most of the country's believers, are the crucial profession that there is no other God but Allah and Mohammed is his prophet; daily prayers (up to five times a day), giving alms to the poor, fasting during the holy month of Ramazan (also known as Ramadan) and making at least one pilgrimage in a lifetime to Mecca.

Like any religion Islam has its range of believers, from fanatical through to conservative to liberal. And it's a religion that reaches into every area of life, which brings special challenges for visitors. If you are a woman it means deciding if you are going to accept Islam's stance that women should dress modestly and thus adopt wearing the shalwar kameez (or a Western equivalent of loose trousers and long loose-fitting shirt) or be a lonely outpost of Western fashion. Personally, I'd rather brave the wilds of the Baluchistan Desert than walk down a Peshawar bazaar in tight jeans and a T-shirt, but it has been done. The result is usually a compounding of misunderstandings that can dog East-West relationships. The more conservative Pakistani men have their misconceptions reinforced that Western women are promiscuous and insensitive and the women (who will often be incensed that they've been pinched, nudged and even spat at) will be convinced that Pakistani men are lecherous barbarians.

I also find it takes a few days to alter my natural impulse to look men in the eyes. Although this won't get you into trouble with men you know (especially if they've already mixed with people from the West), it can be interpreted by others as a reasonably audacious form of flirting.

Refreshingly, though, Pakistani Muslims are happy to talk about their religion. Spirituality isn't considered an embarrassing topic of conversation and Westerners are welcome to visit mosques.

Muslims don't eat any pork products so Pakistan is a bacon-free zone if you are living and travelling with locals. But strangely, although Muslims are not supposed to drink or be able to acquire alcohol, beer and spirits are not hard to come by. Chinese vodka and whisky, locally brewed spirits and wines are in circulation, sometimes disguised as innocent bottles of 7-Up or Pepsi. Or as large cardboard boxes in Kiwi hand luggage.

I'd been asked to bring alcohol in before and had earnt a reputation for being the world's most hopeless amateur smuggler. On the trip before this one, there'd been a plea to bring some Scotch. I bought a small bottle of Johnny Walker duty-free and wedged it in my handbag. 'Don't worry if they do find it, they'll just confiscate it,' I was assured. To someone who feels mortified if they get a parking ticket, this was cold comfort. I replied that although I wouldn't lie about having it in my possession, I would try to smuggle the whisky in.

The Pakistan arrival card I filled in just before landing made no mention of alcohol so I signed it in with a clear conscience. Then came a PA message from the Thai airline steward: 'The Islamic Nation of Pakistan does not allow the importation of alcohol. If you have any in your hand luggage please hand it to one of our crew who will now pass through the cabin to collect it.'

My stomach lurched. Two crew members began to progress slowly down the aisles while I battled with my dilemma. It was all very well to come clean, but I was the only woman on this flight – how was it going to look if I was the sole culprit? Imagine the ignominy of having to unpack the whisky from my handbag. I decided to stick it out a little longer. The steward passed by and I resisted the compulsion to throw myself at his feet and confess all.

I was in sight of the door out of the airport when I finally cracked. Security guards were X-raying every piece of luggage as people left the arrivals hall. My whisky would be hauled out in front of the fascinated and possibly disapproving gaze of hundreds of onlookers. But what else could I do with it? Just before the X-ray machine was a women's toilet. Recklessly abandoning my laden trolley, I dashed in and waved away the bemused elderly woman who was waiting to offer me some sheets of toilet paper. I shot into one of the cubicles, took the whisky out and jammed it behind the loo. I whisked back past the attendant, who was now proffering me a bar of soap, which I also declined. By now she looked simply horrified.

Mujahid was not impressed when he asked where his whisky

was and I pointed back through into the arrivals hall, towards the loo. 'Well, someone will have a good drinks party tonight,' he said gloomily.

So this time I'm feeling quietly smug.

My three friends are loading my bags into the battered ancient office runabout and Mujahid is about to shut the boot down hard on the wine. That 3 litres of wine has haunted me for two days – when I've not been worrying about the box leaking and dripping from the overhead luggage racks in aircraft, I've been cursing the fact it's so heavy or wondering if the Pakistani authorities are going to decide that I'm their starting point for a crackdown on foreigners flaunting the rules. I don't want the damn stuff seeping into the Lahore airport car park.

'Careful!' I blurt, staring meaningfully at the bag.

Mujahid takes the hint and handles it with extreme care. My satisfaction in actually getting the wine here is just slightly blunted by the knowledge that I've gone to all this effort to bring in not some of New Zealand's best but a cheap Aussie red 'chateau cardboard'.

'How much is there?' he asks.

I tell him only 3 litres because I'd had to sacrifice the 2 litres of chardonnay to be able to fit in some clothes.

Mujahid looks slightly disappointed. 'We could have bought you more clothes here,' he says.

mission accomplished

It began here in Murree, my fascination, intoxication, even sometimes a repugnance – a confusion of feelings about Pakistan. It's a town tumbling down the knife-edge ridges of hills that rise from the haze and dust of the plains of Pakistan to culminate in the spectacular collision of some of the world's greatest mountain ranges far to the north. It's taken me nearly 20 years to get back to this town, a mishmash of ramshackle buildings, decay, tacky glitz and honeymoon packages, poignant reminders of past glories, and for me, memories of another life.

Twice before on trips to Pakistan I'd driven past roads leading to Murree, seen the hills behind the capital of Islamabad mounting in misty ranks towards the old British hill station, but had no time to return there. It was important to come here this time – to finally close the circle, see if any old ghosts still lurked among the pines and firs that have survived the steady onslaught of firewood and timber hunters.

I'm standing on the balcony of the Cecil Hotel, an elderly concrete monstrosity left over from the British Raj, its corrugated iron roof so rusted it's a miracle the monkeys that bound over it in the early morning don't fall straight through. And as the crows glide languidly on the air currents rising from the deep gullies, crying like squeaky wheels, I'm caught by surprise to see tears splodged on my notebook. Somehow, since I last heard the crows and the counterpoint of vehicle horns and unintelligible shouts from the bazaar, I've lost the husband I first came here with, gained a new one who's thousands of kilometres away at home in New Zealand and found myself increasingly drawn into the complexities of a country and people I know I will never completely understand. A few tears are probably appropriate.

I'm faring better than the poor old Cecil however. Since September 11 tourism in Pakistan has all but collapsed. There are only two guests – the other one is asleep on one side of the massive bed in my room, wrapped up in a mustard-coloured acrylic blanket printed with a cheetah which is having a violent battle for visual supremacy with the worn maroon carpet.

Mujahid hates Murree so his response on being forced to come here with me is to sleep through as much of the experience as possible. Although he's a Wakhi from the northern areas of Pakistan, a region of mountains so steep the snow can't even stick to the sides of some of them, he says Murree is colder and, what's more, all the businessmen here are cheats.

He also did not enjoy the drive up from Islamabad. It is an hour of hairpin bends interspersed with short straight stretches crammed between shops, tiny wooden stalls no bigger than broom cupboards and tea shops. Traffic along these sections is often reduced to a single-lane crawl. So our driver opted to pass slower-moving vehicles on the bends, even when that involved tight right-hand cornering at speed right in the middle of the manoeuvre. If the truck or bus ahead of us would not pull over to the left, our driver simply passed on the outside. This often afforded me with a stomach-clenching view of the tree-studded hillside below.

Most Pakistani drivers are guided by an unshakeable belief that Inshallah (if God wills it) you will make it safely to your destination, but if He doesn't, no amount of safe driving is going to make any difference. Which is fine for them – the problems arise when I have to drive with someone who is more relaxed than I am about meeting their Maker any minute. And our taxi driver was showing signs that we were in the hands of a man who could put the fatal into fatalism.

As I was in the backseat and could not speak Punjabi, the situation was beyond my control. I had to rely on Mujahid, who was in the front, to remonstrate with the driver. I did vow, however, that if he tried one more outside passing move I would demand to get out. I tried to distract myself by reading road signs. The most arresting was one presiding over a rubbish-strewn hillside: 'Do not distribute litter – this negates a civilised society'.

We shot past a bus with 11 men clinging to the back and even more sitting on the roof. It was not moving fast; the fact that it was still climbing the hill at all seemed a miracle. There were so many passengers crammed inside there wasn't a scrap of daylight to be seen and an assortment of elbows and knees stuck out the open windows.

At this point Mujahid began an earnest conversation with our driver who responded with a quizzical shrug of the shoulders and by taking both hands off the wheel and raising his palms heavenwards. I asked what was going on.

'I have been talking to him about safe driving.'

'Did you get anywhere?'

'No, it is all this Inshallah stuff.'

When we reached the Cecil, our driver, with supreme optimism, offered his services for the next day. Mujahid declined. 'If we had been in the car any longer I think I would have vomited.' And he lives here.

This is the third time Mujahid and I have travelled together. He's a close friend, an excellent guide and he's taken over all my photography – it should be a perfect arrangement. Fuel tankers in Pakistan (of which there are a bewildering number) all bear the warning on the back, 'Danger: Highly inflammable'. This is an apt description of our relationship, which lurches from highly compatible to seething anger without warning as we struggle through a minefield of cultural misunderstandings and misread signals.

We're sharing a room to save money. The receptionist was completely unwilling to do a deal with Mujahid, who unsuccessfully argued that I was just a very small tour party he was guiding. And I'm relieved not to be sleeping in this cavern of a room on my own: for someone who does a lot of independent travelling I've developed an inconvenient distaste for solo hotel stays. Company wards off the spectre of homesickness which I still suffer at night, along with the conviction that I have caught some deadly, exotic disease. I also constantly wake up imagining there are snakes in the room – even in places that haven't seen reptiles on the loose for generations, if ever.

I've never met anyone who can sleep like Mujahid. As I rummage through my pack looking for notepaper he stirs and asks the time. I tell him if sleeping ever becomes an Olympic sport Pakistan will have a sure-fire gold medallist.

'Sleep is good,' he says. 'When you sleep you don't have to bother about women.'

I take the hint and go back to the balcony. The sun is setting and the muezzin in the mosques around Murree are bursting into life. The muezzin, the men who call the faithful to prayer, are in good form tonight. It is the early days of Ramazan and sunset signals the end of abstinence for the day from all food, drink and smoking.

These singers, sometimes competing for supremacy on the amplified airwaves, at other times weaving their calls around each other's in sophisticated harmonies, have rich, tuneful voices. Vibrato tenor notes soar through the thin air (we're at an altitude of over 2000 metres here) and reverberate on the stone walls behind me. 'Allah akbar' – God is great. I remember the comment of a rookie New Zealand journalist who recently went to press likening the sounds of the call to prayer in Pakistan to being stuck in a room with a sick cow. He was either tone deaf or a supreme example of how Western ignorance has contributed to so much misunderstanding of Islam.

For a brief time during the years when Britain ruled the Indian subcontinent Murree was the summer capital of the Raj, a place to escape the almost unbearable heat of the plains. Before Simla took over the role in 1876 Murree was the place where government officials, military personnel, their memsahibs, missahibs and the fishing fleet (young Englishwomen who'd sailed out from 'Home' to look for suitable husbands) would converge to indulge in weeks of balls, dinners and romantic dalliances. The reminders of those days are still here – Holy Trinity Anglican Church on the Mall (with its Sunday school times still advertised), the rustic cottages slowly decaying on the forested hillsides and hotels such as the Cecil.

There's a thick haze over the hills today. It soaks up most of the light from the setting sun. Broken ridges and serrated ranges of hills stretch into the gloom, their jagged edges like badly arranged toast in a rack. Each is successively more indistinct and I can't decide if the faint suggestion of mountains far to the west is really there at all, or exists only in my imagination.

Maybe it's the altitude making me a little light-headed or perhaps it's Ramazan. I'm not a Muslim and Mujahid is an Ismaili Muslim who does not keep the annual month of fasting, but it's difficult to find places to eat during daylight hours so eating and even sips of water take on the nature of an illicit activity. Maybe lack of nourishment is also having a slightly hallucinogenic effect.

The Cecil is perched on a terrace at the edge of which are three small pavilions furnished with wrought-iron chairs and tables. I sit down and immediately begin to shiver: the temperature's dropping fast as the last gasp of November sun suffuses the misty air with gold. To the north are the Karakoram Mountains and some of the highest peaks on earth. The sky in this direction is clearer, and awash with steely cold blues and greens. A small tumult of cloud glows vivid apricot.

Through the Cecil's main door are the reception rooms, their chandeliers probably uncleaned since the last memsahib sailed down the driveway for the final time. The slightly unkempt air adds to the poignancy but the magnificent mahogany staircase is immaculate, its banister silky smooth and sinuous. Double doors open off the deep verandah into our upstairs room, where Mujahid has finally stirred into life and is watching, on the Discovery channel, a programme about crocodiles.

We break open a packet of fresh, golden Iranian dates and consume them steadily and silently for several minutes. They are moist and luscious, a world away from the sad brown fibrous bullets we get at home.

'They are good for your . . . what's the word?' says Mujahid, spitting out a date stone.

'Digestion?' I suggest, having a fair idea it's not what he means.

'No, no,' he says. 'You know.'

'You mean they're an aphrodisiac?'

'An afro what? A food that makes you have good sex.'

How do I get into these conversations? Between us we compile an impressive list of foods that are supposed to have the desired effect. Interestingly, there are few similarities between the Pakistani and Kiwi shortlists. We muse over the possible export possibilities of promoting dates as a low-cost alternative to oysters.

Above us the ceiling has almost disappeared in the gloom. What could be the world's oldest one-bar heater is making no impression on the temperature in here. The ceiling stud must be at least 6 metres high.

Frosted french doors lead to the bathroom, which is like a walk-in refrigerator. There is an ancient bath with an artistic encircling of grimy rings and a thick mat of hair in the plughole. This is one of my pet aversions and any thoughts of a bath are immediately scuppered. One dispirited towel hangs above the bath on a metal rail that I discover is not anchored at either end. When I flick the towel off, the rail comes too, hitting the white tiled floor with a clatter.

'Stop breaking things in there,' Mujahid calls out. I emerge, shivering, and explain that it was the result of a blonde moment. (It was a tactical error explaining this term. From then on I was frequently accused of incidents of stupidity.)

But I am the one who notices the heater's gone off and discover the plug is loose in the socket. I move it to another one and blue sparks shoot out but at least there's a feeble glow from the single bar again. We decide to go into the bazaar in search of dinner, preferably somewhere warmer.

Most people are home indulging in iftar, the snack meal served at sunset that breaks the fast. Down in the bazaar the men who have been frying up the mountains of samosas and pakoras for hours, to be ready for the rush of starving shoppers, have gone home and the carts loaded up with fresh dates (the food traditionally eaten first at iftar) have disappeared.

The Mall, the main promenade where the British would stroll to see and be seen (and where Pakistanis from the plains now come to do just the same thing), is almost deserted. An elderly man wearing a turban with the end draped over one shoulder is pushing two well-fed Punjabi children up the hill in a cart. He's wearing nothing but a thin shalwar kameez and they are clad in layers of acrylic jerseys and padded jackets.

Since I lived here there's been a boom in hotel building. Down from the Cecil is a line-up of empty establishments with marble entranceways and brass door handles. Most are advertising honeymoon packages and iftar buffet meals.

Usually the Mall is heaving with people – Pakistani tourists, locals doing their shopping. I've never seen it so quiet. I people it in my mind with memories from 1984 when I came here to work for a term at Murree Christian School.

Michael and I were boarding parents, caring for 11 teenage girls aged between 14 and 18 whose parents were missionaries or other expat workers in Pakistan and in the Gulf States. We had an Australian, several Americans, two Pakistani girls adopted by Dutch parents, a Pakistani Christian, a Canadian and a German.

I can see them now, arm in arm, heading down the Mall to our favourite restaurant which they'd nicknamed the Cockroach. The interior was slathered in glossy lurid green paint and the only other decoration was the live show of cockroaches that skittered over the ceiling and, presumably in a moment of lost concentration, frequently dropped down onto our table. We braved the wildlife because the restaurant was run by Afghan refugees who cooked wonderful kharai – a rich mix of chicken, tomatoes, peppers and spices prepared in a wok and served with a stack of soft naan bread.

The kitchen was downstairs and if you had a window seat you could lean out and watch the chefs hacking the skinned chickens to pieces with enormous cleavers. Even if you couldn't see the work you could judge progress by the cessation of rhythmic thumping and the hissing gas as the meat hit the oil in the wok.

Every Friday evening at the school we'd discuss where to go for our night on the town and almost inevitably we'd end up here. The electricity supply was – and still is – dogged by power cuts and one evening we were plunged into darkness even before our meal arrived. A little residual daylight glinted off our Pepsi bottles as the stairwell from the kitchen began to glow. A waiter appeared bearing a handful of kerosene lamps which he placed on the tables, bathing the Cockroach in a flattering light.

Michael would be there too, talking to the waiter and rediscovering Urdu he'd long thought he'd lost in the eight years since he'd left the school. As Mujahid and I walked up the Mall I remembered something Michael had said just days after arriving in Murree: 'It still feels like home.'

It is certainly not home for Mujahid, who is muttering about the slim chance of us finding anywhere to eat that's not going to cost a fortune. Thankfully we find somewhere and, what's more, there's a bar. 'You need brandy in Murree,' he says, but his hopes are dashed. There's no alcohol being served during Ramazan. I don't understand why there's any here at all, considering Pakistan's official alcohol ban, although that is more theoretical than practical. But I've never before seen drink so blatantly available.

At least we can eat. A glazed terracotta pot is put on our table: chicken handi. It's rather reminiscent of kharai, only there are no accompanying cockroaches and the flavour is even richer because of its long, slow cooking.

Outside in the bazaar a few people have emerged to walk off the fried iftar treats, and a few doors downhill a man has opened his coffee stall. We buy paper cups of sweet strong foamy coffee for about 75 cents and walk back to the Cecil. Three men are watching television in the reception area. I can never fathom who is actually employed and who are the hangers-on. I can't imagine there's enough work at present for everyone to be on the payroll. We beg two more blankets, arrange for a pot of green tea to be delivered later and ascend the grand staircase to what I've now dubbed The Sepulchre.

The elderly man with a wispy white beard who arrives later with the tray of tea (including two minuscule but tart halves of lemon) is clearly intrigued by our domestic arrangements. The heater is not up to the job of warming the room so we are each stretched out on the bed cocooned in huge acrylic blankets like two giant multicoloured caterpillars. God knows what our visitor is going to report downstairs.

From the bathroom comes mysterious rattling and gurgling from the pipes and a sudden splash of water. We look at each other but are not prepared to emerge from our cocoons to investigate. Mujahid is flicking through the satellite channels and cursing that the best are off the air. But he chances on the start of a movie. Which is how I find myself in what most Western governments consider is one of the most unstable countries on earth peacefully consuming green tea while watching a B grade movie about an American man who turns into a werewolf every night. We're only a few kilometres from one of the world's most volatile borders – you could literally walk into Kashmir (rather heavy military security not withstanding) from here – but I find myself more concerned about how the werewolf can burst hairily from his jeans each night only to appear back home at daybreak in a pristine pair of trousers.

Sleep during Ramazan is a mosaic of awakenings and disturbed rest. The few lights in the bazaar have been turned off as the werewolf finally meets a sticky end courtesy of the family alsatian. Even the indefatigable bus, taxi and truck drivers have stopped leaning on their horns. But not long after 3 a.m. the muezzin are doing their wake-up call, reminding the faithful it is time to pray and to prepare seri, the pre-dawn meal that precedes another day of fasting. This prompts a background hum of activity from the bazaar and the houses crowded on the hilltops and down the valley sides.

I've just drifted back to sleep again when the monkeys arrive, bounding over the roof with heavy-footed crashes, swinging along the wooden lattice balcony outside our room and calling stridently as they do so. When they leave the birds take over, making strange calls that I can't identify. This is frustrating at first, but is it a Western obsession that makes us need to name birds, plants and other objects before they can have real value? It seems an interesting discussion point but the Eastern perspective is still asleep, apparently undisturbed by amplified calls to prayer, monkeys, dodgy plumbing and mystery birds.

After a breakfast of more green tea and leftover dates we hire a taxi to drive to Murree Christian School. I know it won't be open. Only months before my visit two gunmen had appeared in the playground just under the room Michael and I and the girls had used as a lounge, and shot dead six people. Shortly after that the school was closed and the pupils relocated temporarily to Thailand. The killings sent ripples of alarm through the expat community in Pakistan and disturbed the great majority of Muslim Pakistanis who have never condoned violence against minority religious groups. But what got most publicity was the images of Western kids huddled in their rooms, justifiably terrified that they were going to be killed.

The school, on a site now owned by the Pakistani Army but with its old British garrison church still intact, is about a kilometre from the congested Jhika Gali bazaar. Apart from some new flashy hoardings, Jhika looks much the same – the stalls with their pyramids of apples and oranges and mounds of onions and potatoes, and the cobbler who appears to be the same man who restitched my sneakers 20 years ago. I think the tea shop, the first I'd ever been to in Pakistan, is still there but our taxi cannot stop for me to make sure. The road is narrow and two buses are heading straight for us, both trying to shoot the rapidly closing gap between our battered car and a shopfront overflowing with second-hand clothing.

It's moments like this when you learn whether you are a pessimist or an optimist, a fatalist or a control freak. I used to find scenarios like this petrifying but I've become a little more laid back. I don't want to die on a road here but at the same time there's something exhilarating about the audacity of the drivers and the lack of rules.

Today the road is dry and sealed and the dizzying drop on the left-hand-side is now camouflaged with a bright yellow crash barrier. When I first drove along here in a school van that slid slowly into each bend through the mud there was nothing between the churned-up edge of the road and the drop hundreds of metres down to the valley below. Not that the barrier seems to be a complete deterrent to Pakistani drivers shooting over the side. Mangled sections and gaping holes suggest that the Inshallah approach to driving is definitely alive and well.

As we approach one bend I remember a morning walk back from the bazaar to the school when I watched in horror as a small Suzuki van disappeared over the edge at the same spot. We'd been struggling through mud so slippery it was almost impossible to walk without falling over when the van whined up behind us, shot past, skidded and simply vanished. Gruesome sounds of metal grating on rock and snapping trees echoed around the hills. We slithered to the edge as fast as the mud would let us and peered down. There'd been no explosion and we could hear no groaning or cries of agony. The only sound was a lone rock bouncing its way down the gully.

We were preparing to clamber down when the shrubs that blocked our view of the vehicle began to twitch and three young men emerged. They looked up, saw us and I prepared what I hoped was a good Florence Nightingale manner. I need not have bothered – catching sight of me they temporarily stopped their scramble up to the road and rummaged in their pockets. Each produced a plastic comb and carefully rearranged their dishevelled hair and their moustaches. I was flattered but it was also a good indication that all three of them were unscathed.

Today's drive is less eventful – one last bend and the small bell tower of the church building (converted into classrooms many years ago) is before us. But what had once been merely a low wall between road and school is now a formidable red metal fence topped with barbed wire. There's even a sentry box on the corner. A bearded guard carrying an AK47 emerges to talk to us. It is a sad sight, a graphic, poignant reminder of how the world has changed since September 11. Flower sellers (some of whom I'm certain had picked their bouquets of orange and yellow marigolds from nearby gardens), and purveyors of all kinds of other merchandise from shoe laces to plastic toys, Kashmiri shawls and fruit, used to wander into the grounds every day. The school was part of the community.

More than any other event since September 11 and its aftermath, standing in front of the school fortress brings home to me the incalculable damage done to relationships and trust between West and East, and the misunderstandings and fears between Muslims and Christians that have escalated everywhere. Ironically, it was my three-month stay at Murree that had set me on my own one-way slide away from what, until then, had seemed the perfectly reasonable belief that Christianity was the only true religion and that unfortunates who had other ideas were condemned to hell for eternity.

I was 24, had never experienced life in an Eastern culture, never met a Muslim. I watched the men kneeling in the bazaars at prayer time, small boys mimicking their father's gestures, watched Pakistani school girls reading the Koran aloud and began to wonder – guiltily. I was a closet doubter. Although there was a wide range of Christian denominations represented among the teaching and boarding staff at Murree everyone, including me, had signed a declaration of faith. And those articles did not include any provision for Muslims in a Christian heaven, and certainly didn't entertain the idea that their beliefs might be equally valid.

And then one day I discovered I was not on my own. In 1984 the Russians were still battling to control Afghanistan, not so many kilometres to the west. Millions of refugees had flooded into Pakistan and many of these were housed in massive camps on the outskirts of Peshawar in the legendary North West Frontier Province.

I'd spent the weekend with a Salvation Army friend whose husband administered one of the camps. Like most expats (and many Pakistanis) they had household servants. One was a driver called Hajji. He was a Pathan, who looked to be in his 50s but was probably much younger, with a magnificent hooked nose and a beard stained red with henna dye. The name he'd adopted proclaimed he'd made the pilgrimage to Mecca, something all

Muslims are encouraged to do at least once in their lifetime.

On our first drive with Hajji my friend had prayed for 'travelling Mercies'. Considering the standard of driving in Pakistan this was a sensible idea although I could never help but conjure up a mental picture of a carload of black-clad nuns. But on our second expedition it was Hajji who did the prayer – the traditional Muslim prayer for travellers. (This often precedes take-off with Pakistani International Airways and can either inspire confidence or a sense of foreboding. It also explains the local nickname for the national carrier: Prayers In the Air.)

I was astonished – here we were, including my friend's children, being prayed for by a Muslim. As soon as we returned I manoeuvred the conversation around to the prayer.

'Hajji is a wonderful God-fearing man,' she said. 'I trust him with my children's lives every day when he takes them to and from school. I suspect that when I pray and when he prays, we are talking to the same God.'

But when I first arrived at the school I was less concerned with battling the great questions of religion than coming to terms with my first monsoon. My initial view of Pakistan was from the window of a British Airways jumbo that was being thrown around the inside of a boiling mass of monsoon cloud on our approach to Islamabad. Lightning bolts were piercing the gloom on both wing tips and in the row ahead of us a stewardess was pleading with a terrified Pakistani woman to let her strap her baby into a cot for safety. The weeping woman and the sounds of other passengers praying to a variety of deities did nothing to steady my nerves.

The pilot coolly informed us it was the most active monsoon system he'd ever flown through. I didn't want to know this was a new experience for him too. We landed after a series of terrifying free falls, the cabin fittings creaking and protesting and the smell of vomit wafting through the air. I hadn't been sick: my stomach was so frozen with fear that nothing was moving anywhere.

There appeared to be a military invasion in progress at the school. In New Zealand an army presence means a few soldiers eating pies outside a corner store, so it was a shock to see so many soldiers in one place, along with officers in uniforms glistening with gold braid and medals. Badly disoriented, I barely absorbed the information that the army was here for its annual basketball tournament before I collapsed into bed and discovered one of the joys of living in a monsoonal climate: damp sheets, moist blankets, and clammy towels. I wanted to go home.

But over the next few weeks Pakistan began to grow on me like the mould that was spreading out over our bedroom curtains. The routine of school life, the small dramas that erupted in 'our' girls' lives and the challenge of trying to live in close quarters with a group of strangers helped to ease the homesickness. And outside there was the fascination of the smoky tea shops, a first visit to a bangle shop to choose dozens of glittery glass bracelets, the fruit shop wallah cutting open an apple and handing me a slice to try and the sound of the sweeper collecting up the leaves with a twig broom along the path under our window, where 20 years later blood would be spilt, supposedly in the name of religion.

The communal living was a mixed blessing. You never needed to be lonely but it was also an exercise in tolerance or in discovering just how little you possessed. Every Saturday morning Michael and I, together with the senior boys' house parents and any other members of staff who were free, had to meet and view the videos for the evening's film show. Most of the tapes came from the American embassy in Islamabad and the school authorities insisted they were vetted.

I watched amazed and not always silently each week as grisly scenes of mindless violence passed without comment from the American staff who then reeled with horror when two of the characters indulged in an enthusiastic kiss on the lips. This was a moment to be censored. Unfortunately the method of cutting out such unacceptable displays of affection was less than subtle. Most of the teenage audience howled with derision when the staff member assigned to the job would leap up at the appropriate moment and stand in front of the screen.

The guard armed with the automatic weapon breaks into my reminiscing to ask if I want to go back to Jhika Gali to get permission to go inside the gate. I decide not to. I'd need to explain to the one staff member still living nearby that I'm now divorced and happily remarried, but not to the Muslim man who's now looking at his watch and clearly chafing to leave.

But I do try to walk around the perimeter. I can almost see the terrace behind the dining room where marauding monkeys would brazenly steal food from the kids' hands while they ate morning tea. If you stood on a table in one corner of the terrace on a clear day and gazed north you could sometimes see a white peak. I was told it was Nanga Parbat, beyond which the new Karakoram highway stretched all the way to China via the Khunjerab Pass. I vowed when I was in Murree that I would get there one day.

The church is the only building I can see close up. On a school day it was a noisy place, echoing with a pot-pourri of accents, and chairs scraping on concrete. In the evening the central area became our volleyball arena but my most abiding memory of the hall was the night of a concert by a sitar player and his tabala (drum)-playing accompanist.

The whole school was packed into the hall for this rare treat of entertainment from outside. But after two hours the novelty was starting to wear off – in fact many of the six-year-olds were comatose in the front rows and the 18-year-olds at the back were becoming increasingly restive. The musicians showed no signs of stopping and it was clear the senior staff were in a terrible dilemma: did they ask them to stop and thus risk offending them, or simply allow the pile of slumped small children in the front rows to keep growing? The teenagers were not waiting for the adults to sort things out. Two by two they were inventing a range of medical crises and asking to be excused – explanations of everything bar the black death were hissed in my ear by the girls.

While worrying about what so many unsupervised teenagers would get up to while I was still trapped inside, I was distracted by a movement along the beam above the front of the stage. A flying squirrel was sitting there, gazing calmly down at the audience. While the musicians carried on, oblivious, growing numbers of the audience became aware we had company. Maybe the squirrel knew it had attracted a following too, because it proceeded to run along the beams, leaping over the gaps, and occasionally provided ample evidence of the laxative effects of a vegetarian diet.

Suddenly during one of its star turns along the front beam the squirrel stopped, stared fixedly into the middle distance and launched itself into the audience, accompanied by gasps of delight from the crowd. It landed in the lap of the junior girls' house parent, who let out only the faintest of yelps before she bobbed up slightly in her seat. This propelled the squirrel to the floor, where it panicked, darted through the crowd, crawling up legs as it went and achieving what no one else was able to do – bring the concert to an exciting, if chaotic, ending.

It is time to stop looking back. I return to the car where our driver has put on a tape of sung verses from the Koran and is gently drumming his fingers on the wheel. Beside him Mujahid is asleep again but he wakes as I get into the back seat. I'm feeling weepy and blow my nose. He looks at me over his sunglasses. 'That's life.'

Our driver does a U-turn in front of an overloaded bus and we head for the plains.

kalashnikovs and contraband

Thick red brocade curtains are filtering out the white light of a Peshawar morning. But they cannot stop the heat oozing through the windows and washing over my bed. The ceiling fan is scything through the heavy air, beating slowly, like my heartbeat.

The phone rings and I can just hear a languid voice above the throb of the fan.

'Your bus for the Khyber Pass . . .,' he paused, 'is waiting.'

I've been waiting too. For decades I've longed to make this trip, ever since I was first introduced to Rudyard Kipling's swashbuckling tales of the subcontinent. The message might not have the same resonance as being told your camel train awaits but it's good enough for me.

The bus engine is running, not so much in order for us to make a quick getaway as to power the air-conditioning. Unlike rulers and their troops who have wound their way through this harsh landscape over at least two millennia, we will be journeying in relative comfort. But what we do have in common with would-be conquerors such as the Greeks, Persians, Scythians and British is an armed guard.

Ironically our guard consists of Afridi tribesmen whose ancestors made this route such a nightmare for invaders; even today they exert a major influence over this border area. Afridis are just one of the tribes of Pathan (also known as Pushtun) people whose traditional homelands don't recognise the Pakistan and Afghanistan border. Most of these people live in the so-called tribal areas that make up about 25 per cent of Pakistan's North West Frontier Province. In these areas local rulers (called maliks) enforce traditional tribal law and although they at least in theory liaise with the state, Pakistani government authority and laws do not apply.

The tribal areas were established about 100 years ago by Lord Curzon, a British Viceroy of India. They were the British Raj's solution to the ongoing dilemma of trying to control people who simply refused to be subjugated by outside rulers.

Tribal areas are mostly closed to foreigners. One of the exceptions is the road to the Khyber Pass but access is granted only if you have Afridi guards with you.

We have been assigned two and they are already aboard the bus, one riding in the front seat alongside the driver and the other directly behind him. They are both members of the Khyber Rifles, a paramilitary border patrol force that was also established by the British in the 19th century. There's nothing old-fashioned about their weapons. Resting between Mira Jan's and Hyder Khan's knees are Kalashnikovs.

Both men are bearded. Mira Jan's whiskers are white and trimmed closely to match a chisel-sharp nose. Hyder Khan's beard is a more exuberant affair – the tips are dyed with henna and there's more henna-coloured hair emerging from under his black Khyber Rifle beret.

'Does the henna mean he's been to Mecca?' I ask Mujahid.

I get an amused snort in reply. 'No, no. Men do this to cover up grey hair. Sometimes it means they are looking for a wife and want to look younger,' he says, with a touch of pity and the self-assuredness of a Pakistani man with a full head of black hair.

I wonder about asking Hyder Khan if he is looking for a second wife (he's almost certainly got one), then decide a Pathan with a Kalashnikov is entitled to as much privacy as he wishes.

Pathans live by the code of pushtunwali, a complex mix of hospitality, vengeance (most commonly sought over insults or injustices about money, land or women), submission of the vanquished and honour – especially that of the women in a man's clan or family. Blood feuds sparked by breaches of this code are often carried on from generation to generation. There's a proverb in Pushtu (the language of the Pathans) that sums this up: a Pathan took his revenge after 100 years and then said, 'I took it quickly.' Pushtunwali is a system as unforgiving as the land from which it has sprung and yet it is far too simplistic to describe these people as violent or barbaric.

The men might be swift to carry out retribution but they are also quick to smile. A Pathan might never forgive you if you even try to photograph his wife but he'll be in the front row if you want to capture him on film. And they are also great romantics. Although the Pathan armoury of traditional stories is bursting with tales of bloodshed, tragedy and revenge, there are also a surprising number of love stories. Their poetry, too, often deals with affairs of the heart, although it has its own unique Pathan twist. Two of my favourite lines of Pushtu poetry, which to me sum up the complexity of these people, are by a contemporary poet Jala-ud Din:

I am deeply wounded in my heart
From the bullet of my beloved's eyes.

It is impossible to visit these tribal areas, and even the state capital of Peshawar itself, and not be aware of how vitally important guns are to the Pathan men (and the local economy). No man (or boy over the age of about 12 for that matter) would dream of leaving his fortified home without a weapon, maybe even two.

On the outskirts of Peshawar, minuscule shops, their windows thick with dust, display orderly rows of revolvers, pistols and sub-machine-guns.

Most of these weapons come from Darra Adam Khel, a village about 15 kilometres south of Peshawar where, for more than 200 years, gunsmiths have been producing working replicas of just about any gun in existence. There are thousands of people involved in this cottage industry. The gunsmiths use scrap steel, hand tools and primitive lathes to churn out hundreds of guns every day. Replica Lee Enfields, Kalashnikovs, Colts, M-16s, even anti-aircraft guns are made here.

There is no shortage of buyers, even though some of them then have to hire an experienced smuggler to get their weapons through checkpoints at tribal territory borders. (The guns are usually dismantled and the components strapped to various parts of the smuggler's anatomy. The voluminous nature of shalwar kameez makes this a reasonably effective method of smuggling.)

Our bus crosses into the Khyber Agency (the home of the Afridis) 18 kilometres west of Peshawar at Jamrud. Spanning the road is a stone arch that marks the boundary between Pakistani and tribal territory. We stop here and our guards get out with us to chat with another Khyber Rifleman who is on duty. He wants to know if I have a son and if he plays cricket. I can say yes to both so manage to accumulate an armed escort of three back to the bus.

Coming from a country where gun ownership is strictly regulated and even the police don't routinely carry firearms, I should find all this firepower disconcerting. But I hardly like admitting even to myself that I relish the sensation of being outside my comfort zone. Although there is probably very little real danger here for tourists, the suggestion that trouble might be only the twitch of a trigger finger away adds a certain allure.

I'm not the first Westerner to experience this. Many of the British who were posted to the NWFP, including a young Winston Churchill, admired these warrior theologians and poets, even though the Pathans often proved to be deadly foes. Despite the September 11 attacks, Peshawar, because of its proximity to Afghanistan, attracts a higher proportion of overseas visitors than anywhere else in the country, but reports of troubles are few. And the people here are some of the most conservative devout Muslims in the country.

As our bus winds up through the hills into the narrow ravines of the pass the thick haze of the city yields to sharp, cold mountain air. Silhouetted against the sky are Pathan houses which speak volumes about the way of life here. Each family compound is surrounded by thick 3- to 4-metre-high walls of rammed earth. There's at least one watch tower on each property, its sides slashed with gun slits through which the family arsenal can be pointed. Massive wooden gates provide the only entry point. Although the men and boys of the household are free to come and go, it is possible that women in some of these houses will rarely venture outside.

The walls are smooth, with sculpted, rounded edges. They're at one with the hills but at the same time provide a counterpoint to the twisted shattered rock that towers hundreds of metres above us on every side. At its narrowest point the pass is only 3 metres wide. Lookouts and small fortresses made of stone perch on promontories above us. Generations of tribesmen have crouched in these and picked off their enemies toiling up the pass.

Our bus stops in a curve of the road so we can read the memorials to the numerous British regiments that served here during the Raj. The British were the last in a long line of would-be rulers of this region and in 1842 were the victims of one of the most bloody incidents in the Khyber's history. More than 16,000 British and Indian troops were massacred in the pass as they retreated from the Afghan capital Kabul during the First Afghan War.

I know I'm standing on the berm on a modern sealed highway but it is impossible not to be in awe of the fact that the Persian Nadir Shah, Babur (a grandson of Timur [Tamerlane] the founder of the Moghul dynasty) and Darius the Great have all passed by this spot. Even a contingent of the armies of Alexander the Great has trodden this route. Despite what some tour operators will tell you, Alexander himself did not invade the Indian plains through this pass. He sent a small supply force through the Khyber but he and most of his troops marched through a pass to the north, into Chitral and then turned south towards the Indus.

In recent times, though, the pass has assumed more monetary than military significance. The Khyber and the mountains surrounding it are one of south Asia's smuggling hotspots, although this activity has been hampered somewhat by recent events in Afghanistan. And it's not just the conventional drugs and weapons that make their way from Afghanistan into Pakistan to be sold in Peshawar's smugglers' bazaar.

The people of the NWFP are nothing if not practical. The men furtively moving through the hillsides west of Peshawar are just as likely to be ferrying fabric and make-up to the bazaars as smuggling hashish. From the time the British established tribal territories, the local people have been allowed to move goods without paying duties or taxes and this privilege was retained after Pakistan gained independence in 1947. Containers of consumer products are initially shipped duty-free from the port of Karachi under an Afghan transit trade agreement. But almost all of these goods are back in Pakistan in the twinkle of a camel's eye.

As the road twists higher up the pass we meet cyclists hurtling downhill towards Peshawar. Normally, Pakistani men ride upright at a dignified pace but here even grey-bearded elderly fellows are flashing past on sparkling mountain bikes, knuckles gleaming white as they grip the low-slung handlebars for dear life. The bikes are from China, smuggled into Afghanistan. At the top of the pass riders are waiting who will coast down to the bazaar and, Inshallah, into profit.

Pause almost anywhere along the road and in a few minutes you will detect movement somewhere on the hills, such as a small camel train discreetly picking its way east. I spot two figures gingerly negotiating their way around giant boulders that litter the high slopes above us. They have reason to take care. Each is carrying three large square cartons on his back.

'Sonys,' Mujahid says, '21-inch.'

I suspect he's pulling my leg so I get out my camera telephoto. Sure enough, I can read the brand names of the televisions on the sides of the boxes. Later that day he takes me to the smugglers' bazaar to see the shops piled high with televisions that have already made it into Peshawar in one piece. It's estimated that the majority of Pakistani televisions have arrived in the country this way. The bazaar is full of the fruits of the smugglers' labours. There are shops crammed with telephones and I'm certain that in one I can see a small consignment of ex-New Zealand Telecom models. Other shops stock well-known brands of shampoos and moisturisers.

All of it has come directly over the Khyber or via foot tracks in the vicinity.

Donkeys, camels, horses and manpower are all used for smuggling and a lack of pack animals doesn't need to be an impediment. Near the top of the pass we watch police unloading all the luggage from a public bus in their search for entrepreneurs who are using the budget approach to smuggling.

It's not just the provenance of the goods in the bazaar that make it an almost surreal shopping experience. Mujahid is looking for a new telephone for the office and when we open the door of one of the largest telephone shops I'm struck by the curious smell. Unaccustomed to shopping in appliance stores where the staff smoke dope on the job, it takes me a few minutes to realise that both the men behind the counter have been smoking hashish. It certainly makes for a laid-back sales pitch; in fact, one of the assistants doesn't wake up for the entire time we are there.

Back on the pass we reach Landi Kotal, the headquarters for the Khyber Rifles who, along with their border security role, have the thankless task of trying to control the smuggling, something the Pathans believe is akin to a divine right. Although Landi Kotal is not the smuggling mecca it once was since the opening of the new bazaar in Peshawar, it retains a lawless but vibrant feeling. A young Pathan man leaps onto the bus step, miming that we should stop for something to eat. He grins, a flash of pure Pathan animal magnetism framed in the bus window.

There seems to be a higher than average quota of handsome men among the Pathans. I have a weakness for their aquiline noses and piercing eyes, which makes me a hopeless bargainer in NWFP bazaars. Elsewhere I can usually negotiate hard; here it's often a case of one smile from a Pathan shopkeeper and I have trouble not offering to throw extra rupees at him. So I admit that when I suggest Mujahid stop the bus in Landi Kotal I have an ulterior motive: I want to watch the locals close up. And, what's more, the slight frisson of danger is not one I can experience in rural South Canterbury.

Mujahid says no, surprisingly forcefully.

'Why?' I ask.

He pretends not to hear but later tells me that just a few months earlier he'd had an unfortunate experience in the village bazaar. Having convinced two nervous tourists the Khyber Pass was not an especially dangerous place to visit, he'd let them walk through Landi Kotal. They were just telling him that he'd been quite right and how much they were enjoying the experience when only a metre away a Pathan accidentally blew his foot off with his assault rifle.

The end of the road for tourists on the Khyber Pass is the Michni checkpoint. We climb onto a ridge beside a tea shop and gaze down into Afghanistan. Below us a smudge of green vegetation marks the village of Torkham, which is right on the border. Today the air is unusually clear and we can see far to the west where the mountains of the Hindu Kush are still dusted with snow.

Hyder Khan uses his rifle to point out white numbers painted on the mountainsides on either side of Torkham. This is the famous Durand Line, the official ceasefire line between the British and the Afghans settled on in 1893. Like much else in this region, it was achieved only through bitter fighting and bloodshed – the numbers should be painted in red.

But this day the bright light reveals nothing but a few vehicles labouring up from the border. One bus has a horn that tweets melodiously like a bird and the driver uses it at every one of the numerous curves in the road. Birdsong doesn't fit naturally into this environment but at the same time it's typically flamboyant Pakistani.

A gaggle of boys and a few older men gather around us. Not one of them is bareheaded. Some of the boys are wearing embroidered pillbox hats in pink and purple. The older men are wearing woollen hats or turbans. One of the boys takes Mujahid aside and is whispering furtively. I go over to look. 'Hello, nosy Kiwi journalist,' Mujahid says, showing me a handful of grubby, torn bank notes the boy is trying to sell him. They are Russian, a battered reminder that it is not so long since another invader was vanquished by a combination of inhospitable terrain and a ferociously independent people.

We descend to the relative orderliness of Peshawar, Mira Jan reflectively stroking his short beard and Hyder Khan reading my travellers' guide to speaking Pushtu. They have put their guns down. The Kalashnikovs lean against the cool-box beside them, bumping gently against it as we head downhill.

Peshawar might be known best as the gateway to the Khyber Pass but it is also famed for its carpets. Pakistan has its own hand-knotted carpet industry but its buyers also source carpets from throughout Central Asia and Peshawar has one of the best selections.

A most successful dealer is Abid Ali, who is the fifth generation of his family to go into the business. Abid Ali's grandfather moved his carpet enterprise from Afghanistan to Pakistan in 1880 and began selling a range of woollen products from a shop just a few metres square. He later began specialising in carpets and today the family has stores all over Pakistan. There are 70,000 carpets in the Peshawar shop alone so the value of the stock must run into the millions of dollars. There are rugs draped outside the shop, layers of rugs on the floor and rolled up carpets form haphazard ranks at least a metre deep against the walls. Abid Ali says his great-grandfather told him there were three things in life that were hard to find: a good wife, a good horse and a good carpet.

Buying a carpet here is not a matter of browsing among the rolls and unfurling them at will. Carpet selling is a performance art, a carefully choreographed show that has drama, sorrow (when the carpet you fall in love with turns out to be worth more than the family car) and suspense. Abid Ali, his family and staff could win Oscars for their show, which he says is aimed at making clients comfortable and giving them time to choose. What he doesn't say is that the performance also lowers your defences, and mysteriously has all but the most hardened shopper raising their budget.

My show is directed by the impressively built Waqar Samad: clad in a blinding white shalwar kameez, he dominates the sales area. He tells me he is going to show me a selection of carpets simply for my enjoyment and education. 'By the time we are finished there will be a pile of carpets in front of you that comes up to your knees,' he tells me, after installing me on a low sofa and plying me with green tea. His staff, in a perfectly co-ordinated precision display, toss carpet after carpet to Waqar, who unrolls them dramatically in front of me.

He begins with new Pakistani hand-knotted chemical dye carpets. They look good, until he piles on top of them their vegetable dye counterparts. Their more subtle colours have romantic origins – blues are extracted from the indigo plant and the reds from roots of the madder. I soon forget all about the initial flurry of cheap rugs.

Then come the antique vegetable dye rugs, the carpets made of wool dyed from crushed stones and finally antique silk carpets. These are Abid Ali heirlooms that they are reluctant to sell but if I wish . . .

Once the carpets are knee-deep, just as Waqar promised,

the mood becomes more intense. One by one the carpets are removed unless I nod to have them set aside. He seems almost to know which ones I'm going to choose before I do. Clearly my attempt to not show a flicker of interest in any of them has failed.

There's no obligation to buy the ones I have selected, says Waqar. That's just as well, since the first one I point to turns out to have an asking price of $US5,000. I have no intention of buying it, but I am now a marked woman. Once I've made my selection they are spread over the floor.

'Please take off your shoes and walk over them,' he tells me.

I know I'm about to fall into an abyss of credit card debt but I'm powerless to refuse. The sensuous feeling of hand-woven silk on the soles of my feet does the rest. I manage to resist the $5,000 work of art and open negotiations on something considerably cheaper.

'It's a wonderful carpet, Madam.'

'Yes it is. But it's too expensive, I can't afford it.'

'What can you offer me for it?'

And so we proceed until my best price and his are just $250 apart.

'I have compromised many times,' Waqar says in anguished tones. 'Now it's your turn.'

I point out that my compromise is to have doubled my carpet-buying budget in the last 10 minutes. We finally reach an agreement and shake hands.

Nearby another salesman is trying to close a deal with a fellow tourist.

'No, I can't,' the woman says. 'It would mean choosing between a carpet and my husband leaving home.'

The young, handsome salesman shrugs charmingly. 'Well, Madam, a carpet like this is hard to find.'

My carpet has been whisked away to appear a few minutes later rolled tightly and hand-sewn into a tiny hessian bundle complete with carry handle. Abid Ali appears later and asks what I have bought. 'A nice carpet, but I wish you had bought a stone-dye,' he says sadly.

'So do I,' I tell him, 'but I could hardly afford the one I have bought.'

'But it is only money. Buy a better one and send me the money – anytime.'

At this point we are interrupted by a staff member who tells Abid Ali that it's London on the line wanting to know what day to book his limousine for. He's flying there tomorrow for his annual medical check-up in Harley Street. He is not giving up on me easily and rummages among the rolled-up carpets, bringing out the one he wants me to take home. It is gorgeous, with soft hues of blue, green and red. Sulphuric acid has been poured on stones such as lapis lazuli and jade and the colour extracted drop by drop to dye the wool. Abid Ali looks at me almost sorrowfully. He has beautiful eyes – what kind of woman am I to resist? – but I manage to stand firm and ask if he had always intended to go into the family business.

'No, I studied political science and law at university. But there was more money in carpets,' he says candidly, 'and carpets are a very honourable and respectable profession.' Finding the antique carpets, especially the stone-dyed ones, is becoming harder though. 'Our supplies are running out,' he sighs. He glances down at the chosen carpet once more. How did the conversation get back to it again?

A few days later I get an email from my husband. I'd been staying at the former Wali (ruler) of Swat's summer palace since leaving Peshawar. 'I'm worried our credit card number has been hacked somehow . . . If not, did you stay in that palace, or buy it?'

cold meat in a wakhi sandwich

I'm a firm believer in never flying home from a trip without another one in mind.

Likewise, Mujahid also likes to plan ahead so a few days before I was due to fly home after a spring trip to Pakistan he mentioned thoughts of taking an exploratory trip to the desert state of Baluchistan. Would I be interested? It took all of 30 seconds for me to say yes even though I had absolutely no idea how I was going to find the money for another airfare so soon, especially after the severe wound inflicted on my credit card by the Peshawar carpet. But something would probably turn up. This approach makes me the despair of my financial adviser who has suggested that the best way to get me out of debt would be to confiscate my passport for a year.

Several months passed with no news on the expedition and then an email finally arrived: 'How does 10 days in the

Baluchistan desert in December sound to you? I think it would be very good. We will take camels. You will need an armed guard.' It wasn't the stuff of a conventional tourist brochure but it was enough for me. Now all I had to do was find the money, and convince my family that the armed guard was just a dramatic touch thought up by the Pakistani government, and that it wasn't a problem that Mujahid had never actually been to the area before and wasn't exactly sure where we'd be going.

But Mujahid was sure that the Sandy Desert of Baluchistan, which fills the basin between the Ras Koh and Siahan mountain ranges, was the perfect place for commercial camel safaris. Before he started taking proper tourists there, however, a reconnaissance trip was necessary. I would represent potential tour party members and provide feedback: also I was almost guaranteed not to complain if our travel schedule was erratic, or panic if we got lost.

Baluchistan, which shares borders with Afghanistan and Iran, is the largest province in Pakistan and reaches south to the Arabian Sea. It is the country's most sparsely populated region and is the least visited by tourists. In 1999, for instance, fewer than 61,000 foreign tourists visited Pakistan so the number making it to Baluchistan is infinitesimal.

Attempts to develop a Baluchi tourist industry have struck some stumbling blocks. It's still largely a tribal society and the occasional inter-tribal skirmish hasn't helped its image. And, blessed as it is with hundreds of kilometres of Arabian Sea coast and remote, hard to patrol stretches of border, it has been the scene of smuggling on a vast scale. Even the slim possibility of being caught up inadvertently in a shoot-out between smugglers and the authorities has tended to put tourists off.

Now, however, Mujahid and fellow guides felt Baluchistan was a much safer prospect. Taking me there would be one way to put this theory to the test.

While I fondly imagined they were planning the minutiae of our trip I was trying to find ways of paying for my part of it. An organisation called Asia 2000, which provides financial help to New Zealand journalists wanting to write about the region, decided the trip sounded suitably foolhardy to make good reading and provided me with a grant. The remainder of the costs would just have to sit on top of the carpet on the credit card.

Mujahid and I fly into Quetta, Baluchistan's state capital, on a winter's afternoon. Quetta is encircled by mountains so devoid of vegetation that every epoch of their turbulent geological history is laid bare. The Baluchis say that their land was the dumping ground for Allah's leftovers after He'd finished the rest of creation. In geological terms they are not far wrong. Baluchistan was one of the last collision points between the Indian and Asian continental plates, an event that gave birth to three of the world's great mountain ranges – the Himalayas, the Karakorams and the Hindu Kush. Here in Baluchistan the mountains are lower but still dramatic. Multihued strata of rock, twisted and shattered, rear up from the plains, dissected by faults and punctuated with signs of violent volcanic activity.

Quetta has the on-the-edge feeling of a frontier town. It's not a particularly attractive city: an earthquake in 1935 destroyed much of it and the replacement buildings were designed to be functional and earthquake proof rather than decorative. But down at street level Quetta is far more exotic. Not only is there an ethnic melting pot of residents but it is also a stopping off point for nomads, who even today cross international borders in search of new grazing for their livestock. There are the Pathans, Baluchis, Brahuis, Hazaras and Afghans – all with their own languages, turbans or hats, tribal dress and facial characteristics.

As we drive in from the airport Mujahid points them out: 'He's a Hazara – look at his eyes. They are descendants of Mongol troops who fought in Afghanistan'; 'That man in a cap, he's a Brahui'. Then: 'My God, look at those eyes,' he says, momentarily distracted by two exceptionally beautiful dark brown eyes, the only visible part of a woman clad in a full-length black burqa who is standing in the middle of a traffic island. 'Sometimes the eyes are all you need to see,' he says. Mujahid is living proof covering women from head to foot is not going to stop men's thoughts wandering.

The entrance to our hotel is a narrow hall sandwiched between two shops and the tiny foyer is piled high with battle-scarred camping gear.

'Someone's planning a major expedition,' I say.

'They are,' Mujahid replies. 'It's all ours.'

The other two members of our party, Qudrat Ali Shah and Ali Nazar, have travelled from Lahore by train with the equipment and they're recovering from the experience upstairs. Both are cousins of Mujahid's – more Wakhis from the mountains. Their home is in the Shimshal Valley, just a few mountains away from China and, until very recently, the only access from the rest of Pakistan was a two-day walk from the Karakoram highway.

Qudrat is known by everyone as Shahjee, following an incident in Lahore some time ago that involved a foreign film crew, a Pakistani transsexual dancing girl and a police check-point. (It's a complicated story, he tells me, that loses something in translation.) Like almost every man from Pakistan's northern areas he has a smile that could melt the region's glaciers in 10 minutes, a wicked ability for mimicry and a talent for composing songs. Ali is quieter, a thinker, but still there is that smile: seven days in his presence and I'll be permanently cross-eyed. After a few minutes of conversation I know I'm going to enjoy a week in the desert with these two. I'll just have to remind myself now and then that I'm probably old enough to be their mother.

The four of us head out into the bazaar to discuss our travel plans over a meal of sajji, a Baluchi speciality of whole leg of lamb impaled on a skewer and then cooked slowly while set vertically into a bed of charcoal.

There is not another woman to be seen, and all the men are muffled up to their eyeballs in woollen shawls. Outside the sajji restaurant the cooks are lit with a red glow from the charcoal and an elderly man with a straggly white beard is walking past, bent almost double as he pushes a squeaking wooden handcart laden with apples. Despite the fact that I'm almost as well wrapped up as the men, the conversation stops as I come into the restaurant. About 15 pairs of eyes, set above some magnificent hooked noses and bushy beards, regard me with curiosity.

The lamb arrives. It's lightly spiced and served with goats' milk yoghurt. I ask about the travel arrangements while we sit chewing on meaty hunks of bone. It's not a long discussion, because no actual travel arrangements have been made yet.

I must look slightly panic-stricken, which doesn't seem

unreasonable – after all we are leaving for the desert tomorrow.

'Don't worry, it will all happen,' Mujahid says, delicately extricating bits of lamb from between his teeth. So apparently tomorrow we are organising the camels, their drivers, a desert guide and my armed guard – after a seven-hour trip in a four-wheel drive. And we've still got to find the 4WD.

Next morning after breakfast Ali and Shahjee head back into the bazaar to find the vehicle that will take us to Kharan, the town on the edge of the desert in which, Inshallah, all our travel plans are going to fall into place. They return about an hour later, jumping out of the back seat of a double-cab ute. The driver is rugged up against the cold in a chocolate-coloured shawl. (Quetta is at 1700 metres and December is winter as far as the Baluchis are concerned. I'm finding it pleasantly warm during the day.) His companion, who is carrying a rifle and has a bandolier slung across his chest, jumps out of the back of the ute. Our camping gear is heaved aboard and our guard climbs back in, making himself comfortable on top of our packs.

Mujahid, Shahjee and Ali sit in the back seat. I'm in the front and am in charge of catching a plastic gold-coloured ball that keeps hurling itself off the dashboard into my lap. A CD inscribed with writings from the Koran dangles from the rear-vision mirror, the inside door panels are covered in blue glittery vinyl and there are small bells on the brake and accelerator pedals.

To the west of Quetta we cross the Lak Pass over which nomadic shepherds from Afghanistan are leading flocks of sheep and goats. The shepherds have golden skin and almond eyes and their heads are covered in turbans, the long ends hanging over their shoulders. Their animals look thin. It hasn't rained properly here for more than three years: the soil is thirsty and so are many of the animals.

We pass through mountains splashed with sulphurous yellows and ferrous reds, and sometimes interspersed with glistening layers of coal. Some are comprised of rocks so pulverised it's hard to see why they haven't slumped completely to the valley floor.

By late afternoon we reach Kharan, a town that appears to have grown from the earth. Most of its buildings are fashioned from mud – walls and roofs curve sensuously and are topped with whimsical chimney pots. We plan to camp in the rest house compound but the army has got there first. We drive on to the police station to report our presence (because I'm a foreigner my passport details have to be noted down in a ledger that looks as if it has come straight out of Dickens). The senior police officer on duty invites us to stay in the guest house inside their mud-walled compound. We would rather camp outside the town but there's a hint the police would be happier if we would stay where they can keep an eye on us.

The police rest house has an arched verandah along its front facade and domes of irregular sizes erupt from the roof like boils, suggesting the builder either had an exuberant sense of design or spent several heavy nights on hashish before starting work. Mujahid has decreed I will sleep in the tent to be pitched in the compound behind the rest house. When Shahjee and I have pitched it I walk further down the compound. In the far corner the walls are topped with a thick infestation of barbed wire. I go back to find Mujahid and ask him what it is. 'It is the Kharan prison.'

I'm about to ask why I'm the one sleeping in the tent when

the others will be staying behind barred wooden doors of the guest house, when we're interrupted. A representative of the area's deputy district commissioner has come to see us. The DDC, who has heard we are in town, is insisting we move to another guest house. We tell his minion we've unpacked all the gear and put up my tent and we're perfectly happy. But the messenger is adamant – the police guest house is not considered suitable for foreign guests. Although I'm not relishing having to dismantle the tent I'm relieved I won't be sleeping just a wall away from the prison inmates.

Our new home is a modern house in the district's hospital compound. There are signs that someone has been forced to make a hasty exit from the room I've been assigned – a shaving brush in the bathroom and shirts hanging in the wardrobe. My room has a sofa and an armchair and a hospital bed so high I suspect crampons may be necessary for me to reach the top. Because my room has the best range of seating it becomes the reception room for visitors, of which there are many.

First, the DDC arrives in person. He sits on the sofa and discusses our plans with Mujahid who has the armchair. I perch on the bed with my feet dangling some way off the floor. The DDC asks about me but I'm not expected to answer his questions. This is Pakistan and in conservative areas such as this women don't speak to men they are not related to. Mujahid reels off all my personal details. I'm impressed with his grasp of my life history.

I leave the room briefly and am surprised to find our visitor has brought two armed guards with him. They're sitting on a sofa in a room across the hall, watching a lecture about the Koran on a black and white television set. Their automatic weapons are propped against a coffee table. The DDC leaves, telling us his cook will be sending around our dinner. For some reason his guards stay in our lounge.

He's no sooner gone than the assistant deputy commissioner arrives. He, too, is entertained in my bedroom. He's also brought two guards and they settle in with the others. A man Mujahid thinks is the deputy assistant deputy commissioner is our final guest. Clearly there's not a lot of night-time entertainment in Kharan. It appears that he is the previous occupant of my bedroom and seems a little more aggressive in his questioning. I leave Mujahid to smooth his ruffled feathers and note, as I pass by the lounge door, that we've accumulated more armed men. We now have the best part of a platoon watching television and an impressive arms build-up on the coffee table.

Our meal arrives and we eat it sitting on the floor of my room. The guards disappear when our plates and leftovers are removed. I go in search of my sleeping bag. I'd emailed Mujahid a few weeks earlier about this and was told not to bring one all the way from New Zealand; there were plenty in the office's camping store.

'Have you got my sleeping bag in here?' I ask the three men, who are squeezed into the second bedroom.

They look at me blankly. 'What sleeping bag?' Mujahid says.

'The one you said you'd bring me from the office.'

'You didn't remind me about that.'

'I didn't realise I needed to remind you about it.'

'I have many more important things to think about, not just your sleeping bag. You should have checked with me in Lahore.'

'You told me everything was under control. You wouldn't have liked it if I'd checked up on every single thing.'

God knows how my relationship with Mujahid has survived. A combination of being too alike in many ways, and some widely divergent personality traits, has led to some ferocious arguments. Baluchistan will prove to be our make or break trip, but I don't know this in Kharan. It is just as well, though, the weapons have been removed from the next room.

While we are working up to a major conflagration Shahjee is quietly unrolling his sleeping bag and passing it to me. I shift my hospital bed mattress onto the floor. It's such a drop to the concrete from the bed that I'm convinced I'll roll off in the night, break an arm and then I'll be in even more trouble.

Next morning Mujahid extends one of his unique olive branches. 'Seeing you are getting old and forgetful and have no sleeping bag we will go to the bazaar this morning and buy you a blanket.' Equally out of character, I decide to overlook the reference to my alleged infirmities.

Breakfast over, Mujahid begins a long discussion with a gaggle of guards and officials about possible routes for our trek. There is much pointing, drawing in the sand and adamant cries of 'Nay, nay, nay' (No, no, no). I walk out the gate with a cup of tea and watch the sun rise over distant mountains. When I turn around I almost trip over an armed guard who has accompanied me.

Suddenly, in a way I find miraculous but no one else seems to think extraordinary, we are on our way. We have an itinerary and our one police guard turns out to be the owner of five camels. We are going to his village of Zorabad, which just happens to be in the area Mujahid wants to explore. But first we are going to the bazaar for my blanket. I'm told I must stay in the ute because my presence will put up the price. I'm dressed in shalwar kameez and a shawl. Mujahid, Ali and Shahjee are all wearing jeans, sunglasses and each has a Middle East-style headscarf tied around his head. A camel train sways noiselessly past the ute. There are about a dozen camels and loaded on each are metre-high stacks of firewood. The men return – blanketless.

'They thought we were rich Arabs and put up the prices,' Mujahid explains. I point out that as this appears to be the only blanket shop between Quetta and the Iranian border they are just going to have to go back. They return with a Made in Korea acrylic king-size plush blanket. It's bright red and decorated with an enormous peacock in fluorescent orange, blue and pink. I'm comforted by the thought that if we do get seriously lost in the desert and someone organises an aerial search I can spread my blanket out on the sand and even passing satellites should be able to detect it.

It's off to Zorabad with our driver following a single set of jeep tracks through the sand. The people of the village are agog when we arrive. I am the first Western tourist most have ever seen. Babies cry when I look at them, children step back hastily when I walk past. It's a peculiar sensation to feel such an outsider but there's a sense, too, that this is a privilege. This is how the early explorers must have felt and it's something few people nowadays get the chance to experience.

These people are Baluchis. Traditionally they are nomadic herders although today many have settled in Quetta or small villages like this one. They are tribal people for whom family honour and hospitality are vitally important. Anyone who seeks refuge with a Baluchi tribe will be defended to the death. Blood feuds over matters of honour can last for generations and cost dozens of lives. 'A Baluchi's revenge remains as young as a two-year-old deer for 200 years,' says a local proverb. The causes of the feuds are usually zun, zar or zamin (women, money or land).

Baluchi villages have a distinctive appearance. Close together, the dwellings are, in some cases, built like a line of British terraced houses. They are tall – a design feature to protect the occupants against the 45°C-plus heat in summer – and all are topped with decorative chimney pots. Diamond-shaped ventilation holes are cut into the walls: along with the thick wooden doors, these are the only openings.

Outside the houses are shelters made of branches thatched together and supported on tree trunks. These provide shade for the families' livestock. Earthenware water pots are wedged into tripods of branches beside round brick hen houses and each cluster of houses has its own outside tandoor-style oven. At the end of the village, where the dunes are piled up in mounds of wind-sculpted golden sand, is the mosque. Blinding white, it dominates village life but at the same time, over its shoulder, the desert looks ready to move in.

Our police officer Pir Baksh (Forgiven Saint) has gone off in search of his camels. At Mujahid's insistence, he's exchanged his blue police shalwar kameez for his own clothes. The school is opened up for us and our gear piled on the verandah. It is hot and I doze off propped against our packs. When I wake up I'm greeted by a row of fascinated faces: most of the younger village children are standing just a few metres away, transfixed. I hope I haven't been drooling.

Mujahid is playing volleyball with the older boys and their shouts seem to hang in the hot still air. Ali is sorting out his cooking gear and Shahjee is asleep, stretched full-length on top of the tents. Two women fetching water in clay pots from the village well float past us in a heat haze.

And then wending between the houses come the camels led by Pir Baksh, who is soon nicknamed Chacha (uncle in Urdu) No. 1, his son Qudar Nazar, and Budal Khan (whose name means Vision of God), who becomes Chacha No. 2. The camel drivers call 'Ush', the command for the animals to kneel. They do so with much deep groaning and drawn-out bellowing. Two have wooden saddle frames padded with blankets. One, which has a bright blue acrylic rug over the top of a traditional Baluchi woven rug complete with tassels, is 'my' camel.

The three pack animals are swamped by a sea of villagers and camel drivers, all arguing over how best to load them. Mujahid, now wearing his Baluchi embroidered waistcoat, is in the centre of the chaos, yelling instructions. The Chachas no sooner tie one item of gear on before Mujahid is having it untied and repositioned. The scene is reminiscent of the trailer-packing dramas of many a Kiwi summer holiday but with much more dung. Finally, all the gear is stowed on the camels. The last item is a small grey-feathered chicken, squawking in protest, which is popped in among the baggage. Ali is planning chicken curry tonight.

Now comes the moment everyone has been waiting for. A hush falls, dozens of pairs of expectant eyes turn upon me – it is time to get on my camel. What they don't realise is that I've ridden camels before so know what to expect. Camels rise and sit in a series of rocking motions which, for the uninitiated, can be rather alarmingly violent. So when my camel stands up I neither shriek, nor fall off. There is an almost palpable sense of disappointment from the crowd.

We set off, heading west. Pir Baksh is in the lead with his Kalashnikov slung over one shoulder, and his shoes over the other. We are accompanied by many villagers, including a small boy pushing an empty metal wheelbarrow. It squeaks and rattles behind us for some kilometres before its owner turns off our path. The only other human being we see for the rest of the afternoon in this empty land is a turbaned man who is sitting bolt upright riding a bicycle across the sand-dunes. Our camel caravan is moving across land baked hard as concrete by the sun. Its surface is cracked and shiny with salt but irregular plots have been edged with border dykes. If it does rain the water will flood these parched fields and one fall will be enough to see a crop of wheat or melons through to maturity.

After two hours Chacha No. 1 and Mujahid begin to discuss suitable camp sites. As it's winter it gets dark early and they want our tents pitched before nightfall. They choose a place at the base of a ridge of sand-dunes and the pack camels are made to kneel so we can unload them. Their saddles are also removed and young Qudar leads them into the desert.

The chicken is huddling disconsolately beside the kitchen gear. I'm glad for its sake that it won't be spending another day on safari but I refuse to get squeamish about its fate – I love chicken curry. But Mujahid has other ideas for dinner. Before I left New Zealand I asked if I could cook a meal for them and if so what would they like. The reply was 'Bring Italian food' so I travelled to Pakistan with pasta, parmesan cheese, olives, pesto sauce and pine nuts. So chicken was off tonight and pasta was on.

Chacha No.1 and Mujahid take one of the riding camels to a nearby well to get water for us and the camels, Mujahid has commandeered the Kalashnikov and has it slung over his back. A gas lamp is hissing in the mess tent and Ali has cups of tea ready by the time they return. We hear them before we see them: the water is sloshing in the plastic containers that are bumping against the sides of the camel.

Before I begin cooking we all have a fortifying slurp of Johnny Walker Red Label that has been poured into an aluminium mug. (The whisky has come all the way from Scotland via Iran and then by a more circuitous route that Mujahid is reluctant to divulge.) Then, crouched on the sand in our tent, I start to prepare a sauce.

A turbaned figure wrapped in a rug appears in the tent opening. It's Pir Baksh. 'Where is my gun?' he asks Mujahid.

'Oh God!' he replies. Mujahid put the gun down while filling up the water containers, and forgot to pick it up again.

Armed with my miniature torch, which is more suitable for small-scale searches in the bottom of my pack than for night-time expeditions into the Baluchistan Desert, Pir Baksh sets out to find his precious gun. He returns about an hour later and, with a smile that has more gaps than teeth, waves the gun at us. Ali, Shahjee and I suggest he now shoots Mujahid with it. The culprit is oblivious to this. He's fallen asleep. 'No,' says Pir Baksh, 'I will not do that. He is a good man.'

I trudge off to my tent which has been pitched between the mess tent (where Ali will sleep) and Shahjee and Mujahid's tent. Toilet arrangements are simple: there is a great deal of sand out there. I'm not convinced about the warmth of the acrylic blanket so before I encase myself in it like a human sausage roll I put on every piece of thermal clothing I possess. I'm now surprisingly warm. But at 1 a.m. I experience that special phenomenon of desert environments – the massive plunge in temperature from the daytime highs of more than 30°C to something approaching freezing level. I'm shaking with cold. About 10 metres away Shahjee and Mujahid are, I'm guessing, warmly tucked up in their sleeping bags.

I debate what to do. If we were in New Zealand we'd most likely have been sharing a tent to begin with, but this is Pakistan and relationships between men and women tend to work differently. Although my three Wakhi friends are comfortable with Western ways, the Baluchis are not, so for reasons of propriety I have my own tent. As my body temperature drops to new lows, however, I decide that propriety is all very well but it's not worth spending a miserable sleepless night while across the dunes are sleeping bags and warmth. And, what's more, I know my intentions are entirely honourable: I just have a great desire not to die of exposure on my first night in the desert.

But I decide I can at least dress decently for the journey. Our Baluchis are still sitting around their fire so I'm not going to risk offending them with the sight of me in thermal trousers and jacket. So I struggle out of the tent still wrapped up in my blanket. Shuffling across the sands of the Baluchi desert in the dead of night while cocooned in an acrylic blanket the size of Monaco is not easy. But it is nothing compared to the dilemma that faces me when I get to the tent. What the hell do I say? Why has no one thought to install door-bells on tents?

I run through a few options 'Hello, it's me [who else could it be?], can I come in?' or 'Don't get me wrong but can I sleep with you two?' I opt for a discreet cough – no response. I pull the zip on the tent fly up and down a few times but it lacks the necessary volume to make a good door-knocker. Meanwhile the camel drivers have given up all pretence of not watching me. Mugs of tea are arrested halfway to their mouths; they are glued to the unfolding drama.

I finally resort to a plaintive cry that no one has ever let me forget. 'Shahjeeee, I'm freezing.'

There is a rustle from inside. 'Oh my God,' says a voice, the tent zip shoots up and Shahjee's head appears through the opening. 'Come and get into my sleeping bag, I will have the rug.'

He rolls himself in 'Made in Korea' and I thaw out wedged between him and Mujahid. A Kiwi in a Wakhi sandwich.

Mujahid wakes up, possibly because I've accidentally kicked him while I wriggle into my allotted space. 'Did you check the windows of your tent were closed?'

'I thought I had.'

'Well, you can't have.'

I'm still shivering uncontrollably so Shahjee spreads some of the acrylic blanket across me as well.

'I thought New Zealanders were used to the cold,' Mujahid continues. 'Look, I'm not even inside my sleeping bag.' He waves a foot at me.

It's now 3 a.m. and I'm not in the mood for discussing my apparent lack of hardiness. Instead I concentrate on deciding how I will explain this to my husband.

I recounted my desert experiences in a newspaper article when I got home. During a subsequent public speaking engagement I asked if there were any questions. Sitting in the front row was a petite, elderly woman with white hair in a bun and a sweet expression. Her hand shot up immediately. I expected maybe a question on child health, but no. In a voice that could be heard right to the back of the hall she said, 'What really went on in the tent?'

death at sunset

When I emerge from the tent next morning I'm met by the sight of Mujahid, Shahjee and Ali standing outside the mess tent cracking jokes. This is not unexpected, given the events of the night before, but when I join them I discover it's another of my idiosyncrasies that is amusing them. Shahjee points up at the sand-dune behind my tent where the sun is lighting a trail of footprints.

'Were you walking back to Quetta?' Mujahid asks.

The night before I'd decided our Baluchi travel companions were still an unknown quantity to me, so I was not going to advertise my last toilet trip of the day by using a torch. I'd set off up the sand-hill in the dark, taking the torch just in case. Steep dunes are extremely hard to climb at night when you can't judge the angle of the slope. I kept falling over as I clambered to the summit, aiming to disappear modestly over the other side. By the time I came back my eyes had adjusted and I could see my tent easily. Full of confidence I strode down the hill, only to trip over my dupatta (the long shawl always worn with shalwar kameez) and drop the redundant torch.

And now the progress of my night-time expedition is evident for all to see. There was the set of footprints degenerating at regular intervals into a confusion of churned up sand where I'd fallen over on the outward journey and then a dramatic starfish design on the downhill journey where I'd been groping around for the torch.

I'd learnt a valuable lesson – take a less direct route from camp or be teased over the morning cuppa.

After a large cooked breakfast of porridge drizzled with honey and cartoned cream, along with paratha and eggs, we take down the tents and wait for Qudar to find the camels. They've been left to wander the desert munching on the tamarisk bushes that sprout on the sand-dunes and on some subsequent mornings it would sometimes take him several hours to find the camels and bring them back.

Loading the camels is always a noisy process. Chacha No. 1 explains that camels know instinctively when they've been overloaded and, on reaching that point, they simply refuse to stand up. And they let their displeasure known with almost non-stop bellowing. We'd seen this for ourselves when we'd attempted to have two people on each of the riding camels. Normally this would have been an acceptable load but the drought is taking its toll and Chacha's animals are not as strong as usual. They would not budge from the sand until one of us got off.

So, we take turns riding and walking. I'd been warned that

the hard saddles would mean agony on the second day but it was my inner thigh muscles that protested when I climbed on my camel. I was disappointed. Part of my pre-trip build-up had been undertaking my gym's first ever programme designed for someone going camel riding. (I'd also dragged my husband out into the wilds behind our town so that I could practise toilet stops. 'Can you see anything?' I'd bellowed through the trees. 'No,' came the reply, 'but the bus load of Japanese tourists behind you have their cameras out.')

The camel's swaying gait is also hard on the lower back. Mujahid, who is riding the other camel, passes me, and points out that the motion is not unlike sex and therefore has aphrodisiac properties. I suggest that these would be cancelled out at night by the agony of aching muscles, and the aroma of camel that hangs round us and the bedding.

Skeletal remains of goats, and sometimes even camels, lie partly submerged in the sand along our route, a sombre reminder that even creatures so well adapted to life in this harsh environment eventually reach their limits of endurance. Pir Baksh tells us that most of his camels have died during the drought and he may sell these last five. He is tired of the worry of trying to keep them alive. He no longer shoulders his gun. It's slung over the back of my saddle. He must have decided the chances of needing it in a hurry are negligible because he's removed the working parts (tucking these in his shalwar kameez) and wrapped plastic bags secured with string around the rest of the weapon to keep out the sand.

Our progress is often silent as the camels' splayed padded feet make no noise in the sand. Occasionally there is a muffled cluck from the chicken; its head can just be seen poking out from the luggage on one of the pack camels. We can see the smoky blue heights of the Ras Koh and Siahan Mountains to our left and right, and between them and us stretch wave after wave of sand-dunes and rocky escarpments.

The colour of the sand changes during the day. It's cold grey before dawn, the colour of ripe apricots when the sun hits it, tawny gold at noon and at sunset becomes molten.

The dunes themselves are rippled with wavelets of sand that throw shadows as fine as paintbrush strokes. On the large dunes the shadowed faces are like black pools, their surface interrupted only by the blue-grey tamarisk trees that hang like wisps of smoke over the sand. These trees are the camels' only food (apart from our meal scraps) and they greedily snatch bites at them as we ride past. At lunchtime they crunch on the branches as we catnap nearby. We often see other camels grazing on the trees or standing against the skyline gazing into the distance. They all have owners, Pir Baksh says, but usually there is no one in sight.

That night we camp beneath a sinuous ridge of sand-dunes surrounded by rock-hard salt pans. Shahjee appears at my tent, gives me his sleeping bag and takes away the blanket. As we finish organising the tents Ali hands me a cup of green tea and issues some instructions. 'You can go and watch the sunset from that ridge,' he says, pointing up to the razorback of sand above us. 'It would be a good idea to go now.'

'I'll just . . .' I start to say.

'Please go now,' Ali interrupts.

I'm a little puzzled; Ali is not given to ordering me around. But I slog up the dunes, to be joined by Mujahid shortly after. He's preparing to take some sunset photographs when we see a man wearing a flowing white gown and a crocheted white cap climbing up from the other side. Behind him are two more men in embroidered caps and shalwar kameez. Until then we had no idea there was a village nearby but can now see the outlines of houses several ridges of dunes away.

The visitors squat down in the sand near me and begin to ply Mujahid with questions. Although they are talking to him their eyes never leave me. Every time I move they swivel to watch. This does not usually worry me but for some reason tonight I find the scrutiny too intense. That is why dupattas are so handy. I rearrange mine over my head, looping the longer end over my shoulder, thus shrouding my face from anyone who is not standing directly in front of me. They seem to take the hint and shortly after abruptly stand up, say 'Khuda hafiz' to Mujahid and head home.

As soon as the sun has set we follow suit and I discover why Ali was so adamant I should go on my outing. A pressure cooker, steam whistling out its top vent, has been placed on the gas burner. A small smear of blood on a rock outside the mess tent signals chicken curry is on the menu. Ali was obviously taking no chances that I might have an attack of hysterics witnessing the execution of our feathered travel companion. Later the three of them fall about laughing when I put my hand down on the chicken feet one of them has placed near my eating spot in the tent.

Next day I spend two and a half hours without a break riding my camel. We are moving through a small pass between the dunes and I'm longing to get down. Everything is aching and I'm afraid that if I can't dismount soon I'll simply topple over one side as my muscles seize up.

'I think I need to stop,' I tell Mujahid who's walking nearby. He stretches his arms and wiggles his hips. I'm mystified until I realise he's listening to my tape of Westlife on his Walkman. I throw my bottle of water in front of him to attract his attention.

'What?' he says, clicking off the tape.

I explain I'm in agony.

'Just wait a little longer. It will be worth it.'

We round a slab of rock and before us a ridge of dunes rises 100 metres above the valley floor. At its foot is a smudge of green – an oasis. I forget the stabbing pains down my left leg as the camels quicken their pace, eager to reach the water. Palm trees and tall grasses grow in the sand. Donkeys and sheep with remarkably fluffy white wool considering the harsh environment, are grazing among them. Life is imitating art. The Baluchis have a saying to explain how camels are often left to their own devices but other animals are better cared for: 'If you see a donkey, you've found an oasis, but if you see a camel you're lost.'

The sand-dunes tower above us. A black crow perched on a ridge is the only foreign object along the mountain of sand. Beyond the palm trees is a well. Two men wearing ankle-length gowns are drawing water using a spool-like wooden wheel. When the bucket, made from a tyre, reaches the surface a third man leans over, grabs it and empties it into a long ditch with curved earthen sides. Dozens of camels are crowded round this, jostling for position. It's a timeless scene. I stand near one of the grey-bearded men winding the wheel and feel as if I've walked into a scene from the Old Testament. He looks at me as if I've materialised from the moon.

While I watch water slosh into the ditch a herder and his

camels appear over a rise. The youngest animals begin to gallop down the slope, their gangly legs going in all directions, an ungainly buck or two interrupting their progress. They may have been more than a week without water. Chacha No. 1 tells me that in winter camels can go 10 days without a drink, but in summer their limit is three days.

We sit down under the palms and eat cheese and two packets of biscuits. Pakistanis love biscuits and the selection is vast, everything from 'saltish' to cream-filled and sesame seed-flavoured.

A walk into the vegetation reveals that the plants are not left entirely to fend for themselves. Many have circular mounds built some distance from their trunks and I watch as a small boy staggers from the well with a bucket of water and pours it into the ring.

We leave the oasis as the sun begins to slip down from the sky towards the dunes. Mujahid turns around in the saddle of the lead riding camel, looks back at the oasis, and raises one arm in the air and shouts, 'Pakistan zindabad!' (Pakistan forever). The three men from the mountains love the desert. They find it hard to say why. Maybe it's the silence, the clean air and the lack of people (they spend a lot of time in Pakistan's packed, chaotic cities). Maybe it's the lack of complications out here. All of them are responsible for large extended families, including elderly parents and young children. In the desert there's at least a reprieve from the worries that come with this role.

I have with me a book by Kurban Said, an author of mysterious origins who, in the 1930s, wrote *Ali and Nino*, a love story about East meeting West during the First World War. One of the book's characters suggests that the world is divided into two kinds of people – wood men and desert men. While we are sitting around the fire that night, watching the Chachas cook their huge ovals of bread in the embers, I read out a section from the book. 'The Orient's dry intoxication comes from the desert, where hot wind and hot sand make men drunk, where the world is simple and without problems. The woods are full of questions. Only the desert does not ask, does not give and does not promise anything.'

There is a silence. We've all come to the desert with emotional baggage of some kind. There are family worries and, for the men, women trouble. At home my father is very slowly fading away after a severe stroke. This is one of the few places on earth where any means of contact with the outside world is days away. I'm powerless to do anything and wonder aloud at the feeling of relief that comes from being temporarily removed from the stresses of ordinary life.

'You should try not to feel too sad about your father,' Mujahid says, his hands extended over the fire. 'He has reached a good age. It may be time for him to go.'

This attitude, so different from the prevalent Western view that people should be kept alive at all costs, is like a gentle breeze blowing down from the dunes. Unlike me, Mujahid and his cousins have seen death before. Materially they might have more than the Baluchis, but life is hard in the mountains and death is ever-present. Mujahid is still coming to terms with the death of his younger brother, Ali, who was crushed by rocks as he was building a retaining wall on the family's land. Ali left behind a young widow and a baby son. It is now Mujahid's responsibility to look after them.

Above us, a satellite is moving west towards Afghanistan.

It's hard to grasp just how remote we are and yet, less than a year later, this same air space will be alive with American bombers, spy planes and other aircraft. No part of the world, it seems, can ever truly be a backwater.

When I glance back around the fire I'm startled to see an extra figure sitting in the shadows beside the Chachas. Out of the darkness has come a nomad who has been searching for one of his young camels. He saw our campfire and now he and Pir Baksh have begun a unique Baluchi custom, the hal. When two Baluchis meet, even if it is only after a short time apart, they must give each other a full account of everything that has happened to them since. This can mean some long conversations but it is also an effective way for a nomadic people to gather up information about the conditions that lie ahead, especially the whereabouts of water.

Tonight I'm sleeping on top of a sand-hill far removed from the others. My tent has been consigned to the wilderness because I've developed a cough at night, and a blocked nose. The latter, according to Mujahid, is making me snore. So in order to preserve his beauty sleep I've been banished out of earshot. I'm not worried about being marooned in the dunes until one of the camels wanders too close during the night and tweaks one of the guy ropes. I lie awake for some time after that thinking about the oasis. Images of the lime green light cast by the palm trees, the sheep rustling through the grasses beneath and the camels drinking long and slowly at the well will never leave me.

In the morning we discover the oasis has had a less picturesque effect on our camels. All five have rampant and explosive diarrhoea. A foul miasma hangs over the caravan, and the desert peace is punctuated with almost continual camel farting. They didn't mention this in the romantic tales of Lawrence of Arabia and the Foreign Legion. When Shahjee turns around on his camel and shows me how he's fashioned his scarf into an emergency gas mask I'm reduced to helpless giggles. Usually those of us taking turns on foot keep close to the camels so we can walk in their shade. But today we're keeping our distance and when my jacket falls off the back of my saddle into the path of the pack camels we hold our breath. Luckily the camels temporarily restrain themselves as they step over it.

Today we are planning to camp near the village of Niko. Our route takes us across the dry bed of the Baddo River. When this is flowing it drains into an extensive marshy area to the west, near the Iranian border. It is hard to imagine, when looking at the arid, almost lifeless landscape around us, that a farmer here can convert 100 kilograms of seed into 10,000 kilograms of crops – most commonly wheat, sorghum, aniseed or water-melon – if only he has water.

At the junction of two parched river beds is the village, three one-room cottages joined together and protected by a single thatched roof; a few smaller detached buildings and a thatched shelter for the livestock. Parked outside one of the cottages is a gleaming 4WD. This belongs to a game ranger who works for an Abu Dhabi sheikh. The area is popular with Arabian visitors who bring falcons to hunt for small birds among the dunes. The hunting can't be good at present: with the exception of the black crow at the oasis I haven't seen a single bird. Ali, who has worked in the Gulf States, tells me that when the sheikhs come to Pakistan to go hunting their falcons travel in first class along with their owners.

The village is new. The families moved here in the hope of

finding a reliable water supply after the well at their last home ran dry. They have sunk a well nearby and at 25 metres hit water, only to find it was brackish and undrinkable. Slowly their animals, their only remaining source of food and income, are dying. If it doesn't rain soon they may have to join the hundreds of other semi-nomad families that camp outside towns like Kharan and even on the outskirts of Quetta.

We turn off up another dry tributary and into a landscape that feels more lunar than earthly. Shattered rock forms the valley sides and the afternoon sun is a glancing blow off the river bed. If a spacecraft from *Star Wars* had borne down on us I would not have given it a second look.

At the head of the valley we cross a mountainous pile of sand and the camels jog down the other side, all of us looking expectantly at the well at the base. Pir Baksh goes on ahead and we wait for his signal. The animals are restless and demonstrate frequently that their digestive systems are still not happy. Pir Baksh has turned his back on the well. We can tell without asking that there is no water. There are only a few hours of daylight so we have to keep moving till we find some.

We head across a vast plain between the sand-hills. In the distance a shepherd is leading his small herd of brown and black goats in the direction of the dry well. Pir Baksh sets off to intercept him. We think we can see them talking but it is hard to tell. They are shimmering in the heat haze – the goats appear to be floating several centimetres off the ground.

Our camels plod on. We might not have water but there is almost no danger of getting lost. Pir Baksh is known throughout Baluchistan and beyond as a khoji or foot-tracker, because of his extraordinary tracking abilities. At night the briefest flicker of a lit match over the sand is enough to give him vital clues about the way ahead. He is sought after by police throughout the country, not just to hunt criminals, but to find stolen animals: he can recognise the footprints of individual beasts. Qudar sets out for home earlier than us and two days later Pir Baksh stops at what in the desert passes for a busy intersection. There is no one else here, but two tracks intersect and there are many footprints. He leans down and immediately points out his son's. He tells us that if he is shown any parent's footprints he can recognise those of their children.

At the head of this valley we hear a rare sound – a motor vehicle is coming. Lurching over the hill is a blue ute, its deck piled high with a motley assortment of water containers and its cab crammed with men. Pir Baksh and Mujahid stop to talk to the occupants.

I can't understand Baluchi but I enjoy listening to it. Sentences always seem to end on a high-pitched note which makes it sound as if the speaker has just sat on something sharp. Mujahid, Shahjee and Ali spoke no Baluchi when they arrived in the desert but after just four days they are communicating with our Chachas in a combination of Urdu and Baluchi. They reckon that, given a month in the area, they could understand at least 50 per cent pure Baluchi.

The Wakhis have an astonishing ability to pick up languages. Mujahid speaks Wakhi, Urdu, English, Punjabi, Pushtu and Burushashki, a language from the northern areas said to originate with officers of Alexander the Great who had stayed behind in the 4th century BC. He's also fluent in German, speaks good French and can understand various other Pakistani dialects.

The ute drives off. The news for us is mixed. The well we are heading for has water but the pump is powered by a generator, the pumphouse is locked and the operator is nowhere to be found. The ute party will try their luck elsewhere but we must keep going. In the distance we see the pumphouse, an incongruous concrete cube set down in a world of sand and earth. A ditch beside the well is used as a drinking trough for animals but there is little left for our camels to drink. Still, the decision is made to stop and wait to see what happens. Maybe the engineer will arrive, Inshallah.

The sun is beginning to set when a motor cycle appears. It has orange mudguards that stick out like ears from each side and both are decorated with painted eyes. Tinsel dangles from the handlebars. Its young rider dismounts and takes a set of keys from his pocket. He is the first person we've met in the desert who is not at all fazed by the sight of one Western woman in dusty local garb and three men all wearing Arabian headdress and wrap-around sunglasses.

The pump engine roars to life and the tank outside starts to fill with water. Our camel drivers begin bucketing water into the ditch and the camels splay out their front legs and slurp up the water. Once we have set up camp nearby, Mujahid, Shahjee and I go back to the well. Using the rubber bucket that has a disconcerting habit of changing shape when it's full of water, we pour tepid water over each other's hair. It's the first shampoo mine has had for a week. Not that I've been worried – the desert seems to refine one's priorities and daily washes and hair- and skin-care have not been at the top of my list.

Despite the utter peace around us, Mujahid and I have managed to bicker ever since the journey began. The tensions boil over at the well.

'If I said the sky was blue you'd say it was red. Don't be so bloody difficult.'

'And you should spend more time listening, not talking,' he replies.

I'm almost overwhelmed by an urge to push him into the muddy ditch, and no doubt he'd like to do the same to me. A herd of goats looks on with strange vacant eyes as we call a truce and wash some clothes. We see our camels walking along the top of a dune above our camp, their shapes silhouetted against a burning sky, their shadows stretching far down the sand.

Singing is coming from the mess tent as we arrive back in camp. Ali is cooking and providing his own musical accompaniment. But he's not happy with the water, and tells me there will be no green tea that evening as it tastes 'saltish'. Next morning I'm surprised to see him standing outside the tent holding a cup of coffee for me.

'I don't think I'll be able to drink it, but thanks for trying,' I tell him.

'No, no, it's okay. Try it.'

I take a sip. It's fine. In fact it's delicious.

'Have you used mineral water?'

Ali grins and rummages among his supplies at the back of the tent. He pulls out the bottle of Johnny Walker. So, either whisky has a little-known ability to neutralise salt or otherwise there's so much alcohol in my dawn drink that I'm incapable of detecting the salty water.

After another day loping over the salt pans and dunes we are nearly home, back to Zorabad after our loop through the Sandy Desert. I have been the first Westerner to visit some of the villages on our route. I've also left many preoccupations behind in the sand: it has not been just a physical journey, but a journey for the soul.

Next morning I'm woken by Mujahid offering me a cup of coffee. 'Come and see the dawn.' Outside a scud of clouds is caught by the rising sun. They are flushed rose pink and the sand is beginning to glow beneath a sky the colour of mother of pearl.

Mujahid gives me a hug. 'I am sorry I have been a bastard. I have many problems.'

I say I'm equally sorry I have not been more understanding.

He goes back to taking photographs of the sunrise. Suddenly he stops and throws his arms wide. 'Thank you, God, for letting me come to see your beautiful world.'

This time I have no argument with the sometimes infuriating Wakhi from the mountains. The damned man is right.

running hot water

An argument is bubbling away in the back seat of the double-cab ute as we wind through the Bolan Pass. The pass cuts through the Brahui Mountains south of Quetta like a wound. It is a place with a violent history but there is nothing academic about the discussion behind me.

Because I'm the only woman I'm in the front seat, with two total strangers, while Mujahid, Shahjee and Ali sit wedged in the back. We've been travelling for several hours since leaving our camels at Zorabad and the mission now is to find the side road that will take us to Pir Ghaib, a place I've been told about on a previous visit to Pakistan and am curious to see. Pir Ghaib (The Vanished Saint) is an oasis. After a week in the Sandy Desert where almost the only running water has been the half-litre poured into my washing bowl each morning, the word has taken on almost mystical qualities.

This is no ordinary oasis either. Pir Ghaib is a hot spring that gushes from the side of a ravine – the water cascades to the valley floor through a series of pools. I've been promised a swim but as the shadows in the gorge gradually swallow up the remaining light I can't see it happening today.

Where the side road is supposed to be, according to Mujahid, is a quarry of medieval appearance. Men in tattered shalwar kameez, their black hair coated in white rock dust and skin ghostly grey, are dragging wheelbarrows up and down rock piles the height of a four-storey building. Near the base of one of the shattered mountains of stone a group of men squat in a circle, bashing rocks into pieces. A pall of dust hovers overhead.

Mujahid decides we must go cross-country, pick our way through the dry river bed and link up with the road somewhere on the other side. Shahjee is convinced that the side road is still here, but on the other side of the quarried rock mountains. But Mujahid prevails and off we bump, the ute pitching and graunching across the river bed. Our driver looks about 14 and it's soon evident most of his driving until now has been on sealed roads. He's hunched over the wheel, muttering in Baluchi, and seems to have no idea how to pick out the best route over terrain that looks more suitable for roped mountaineers.

On both sides of the river are mountains streaked with colour but so disintegrated and raw it seems impossible they are still standing. We seem to be negotiating our way through a fossilised game of giant marbles. The three from the back seat are now walking in front of the ute, heaving boulders the size of large fridges from our path. I want to get out too, but I'm told to stay in the ute. I'm having great trouble not ending up in the lap of the driver's mate as we bounce from rock to rock. He looks like the sort who could get the wrong idea, but either I preserve my honour and hold onto the dashboard with both hands, or keep a grip on my camera. I opt to protect the latter.

We come to a shuddering halt, faced with a sea of boulders ahead and no sign of any track. The sun is rapidly making its getaway behind the ridge to our west and if we don't get out of here soon we'll be trying to drive up the steep twisting road to the oasis in the dark. But Mujahid is not going to give up. We reverse over several metres of hard-won territory and veer off in a slightly different direction. I've stopped worrying – nobody else seems greatly perturbed so it seems pointless. And then, just as we spot the track ahead of us, another ute appears from the quarry on our left, driving unfalteringly along the road across the river bed that was just where Shahjee said it would be. No one says a thing.

I assume the worst is over as we drive towards a smudge of green ahead which I guess is the oasis. But it is a lower village, date palms punctuating the mud-walled homes and fields like exclamation marks. We weave our way through a herd of cattle being driven home by barefoot children armed with sticks, the dust that swirls around them turning golden in the setting sun.

The track then starts to climb a ravine and our driver develops a look of real panic. I'm sure he's never driven up a road like this before. Instead of giving the ute some acceleration he lets it stall on the steep parts and we start rolling downhill. I fight the urge to tell him I'll drive. Great slabs of the road have fallen away in places and the ute only just edges past the drop. Ahead lies a tight bend around a bluff that plunges down to the valley floor. The outer metre of road is already down there. I get out.

I recognise a rising tide of panic that strikes me only when I'm tired and am a long way from home. What am I doing trudging up the side of what seems like the world's largest geological disaster area? The mountains had looked fascinating this morning; now they are simply menacing.

The Pakistanis believe the spring is the visible reminder of Pir Ghaib, a beloved local Sufi saint who, together with his sister, had been preaching Islam in the area. Legend has it that they'd angered some of the inhabitants who had pursued them to this spot. Pir Ghaib's sister was killed by the rabble but he escaped, disappearing into a small cleft in the rock. He was never seen again, but hot water immediately began to spring from the cavity.

Looking around me I can appreciate Pir Ghaib's fears as he fled his attackers, but my reasons are geological rather than spiritual. If the saint hadn't created the thermal springs I'm betting tonight's chapattis they were the result of water being heated up far below us along what could be a very active fault line. Faults mean earthquakes. Above us boulders perch precariously on crags, and great slabs of cliff are slashed with gaping clefts.

Somehow the ute makes it round the last of the hairpin bends and we are reunited at a mercifully flat area near a mudbrick house. A man of indeterminate age appears with two small children and leads the way to the guest house. Somewhere below us is the tantalising sound of running water but before we can check out the springs we have to unload the gear. All of it, Mujahid says, even the camping gear we won't be using: 'It is not a good idea to leave anything in the ute.'

'Why?' I ask.

'Always questions, questions,' he says, heaving a tent over his shoulder. 'Never again, a Kiwi woman journalist. There could be bad people around here.' He waves a hand around the amphitheatre of rock.

So we carry all the contents of the ute to the guest house. It is a somewhat grandiose title for the concrete building tucked among palms and boulders that have spilled down the cliff face, maybe hundreds of years ago, maybe yesterday. The front and back walls of the shelter are open, and at either end are two rooms with barred windows and metal doors fastened with massive padlocks. The chowkidar opens one of the rooms and we pile our gear inside.

'You will sleep in here,' Mujahid says.

'Where are you all going to sleep then?' I ask.

Apparently the men will sleep in the open section.

I look around the concrete cell with its barred windows. 'I'd rather sleep out here with all of you.'

'No, it's not safe. When you go to sleep we'll be locking the door,' Mujahid says. He won't elaborate. I consider asking why, but one look at his face stops me. Maybe it's the 'bad people', which I'm sure is a Mujahid euphemism for everyone from petty thieves to rapists and murderers. But nothing could be worse than being locked in this concrete cell and hearing an earthquake rumbling underfoot.

Ali begins cooking dinner and in the dying light Mujahid leads the way to the springs. Long grasses, oleander bushes and palms have found footholds around rocks through which streams of warm water flow. At the cliff face the water spews from the hole in the wall, the last hiding place of the Vanished Saint. Usually there is much more water, Mujahid says, but because of the three-year drought even underground water supplies have dwindled.

The water near the mouth of the cave is steaming and clear but although this is a venerated spot, the surroundings have been strewn with rubbish. It is heartbreaking. It seems acceptable to drop rubbish (there are no litter bins anyway) and of course no toilet facilities. After my initial terrors over toilet trips in the sand-dunes I'd soon adapted, but this is far, far worse – nothing but a hillside of boulders, and plenty of people have been here before me. By the time I stumble back into the shelter Ali's curry is boiling and he is slapping out the chapattis. The graffiti scrawled in Urdu script on the walls flickers in the light of the kerosene lamp. Mujahid, Ali and Shahjee talk cheerfully. Sitting on the edge of the light and out of the conversation I'm awash with loneliness and suffering a bad case of traveller's jitters.

We eat dinner while the chowkidar's children stand outside the ring of our lamp and watch. They are hungry and Ali gives them a stack of chapattis and curry. The men tease the kids as they scoot away with their dinner. I like the way Pakistanis help each other. Ali's sharing of our food with the kids is a natural, practical act, he doesn't expect to receive admiration from onlookers.

Apart from the sound of the stream there is absolute quiet at Pir Ghaib. While I am trying to pull myself together there is a rattle of boulders behind the guest house and five goats leap the low wall and charge into our midst. The ringleader, a tall rangy white animal, glares at us with his mad yellow eyes before Ali throws a pot lid at them and they clatter away. But these are either the most desperate or the most evil goats in the East, because they refuse to give up. The evening is enlivened by shouts in a variety of languages, the clang of metal cooking equipment being flung across the concrete, and the goats from hell galloping around the building.

I am sent to bed in the cell while Mujahid, Ali and Shahjee settle down in the shelter, each with a tent pole beside them to fend off the goats and, as some kind soul tells me, the packs of wild dogs that sometimes range the hills. I huddle into my sleeping bag beside the tents that smell vaguely of camels and hear the voice of a colleague at work: 'Why can't you just go to the Gold Coast like ordinary people?'

The wind rattling the palm fronds wakes me in the morning. Then I peer up at the window facing the stream and see two heads silhouetted against the dawn. The chowkidar's children are standing on tiptoe looking through the barred window, discussing me in loud whispers. 'Salaam aleikum,' I croak at them and they vanish.

There are signs of life from the verandah too. I know the men had a disturbed night because I woke several times to see torch beams strafing the ceiling and heard the clang of pots as the goats made daring early morning raids on the camp. The bolt is dragged back and Mujahid appears. Fed up with the goats Ali has decided to cook breakfast in my room. I stay in my sleeping bag and am fed French toast cooked on the nearby burner. Things are looking up, or maybe it is the slug of illegal whisky in my coffee.

Shahjee and Mujahid set off to climb a bluff on the far side of the stream to take photos while the light is good. I am given instructions about which pool to use for the long-awaited swim. 'We will sit on the hill and be your guard,' Mujahid tells me. Yeah, right. Swimming is not a common activity among adults in Pakistan, especially not for women outdoors, so my dip has to be planned carefully. Idyllic though the surroundings look this morning, there'll be no cavorting in the pool au naturel.

Clad only in a swimsuit, sarong, towel and a jacket, I wind my way down the side of the cliff to the pool. It is surrounded by palms on the lower side, with an almost sheer rock face on the uphill side. Down this tumbles a small waterfall. The water looks clean but, given what I and every other pilgrim for years have been doing on the rubble a few hundred metres above me, drinking from the pool may not be a good idea. I have no idea if it is safe to put my head under either. Various news stories about people dying of meningococcal disease caught in hot springs start bobbing around my brain.

But I desperately want a wash and to rinse the quantity of Baluchi sand from my hair so I wade into the lukewarm water and, once up to my neck, unwind the sarong and fling it onto the bank. As I made my way down the path Mujahid and Shahjee had waved from their vantage point on the cliff face opposite and now there is the sound of distant cheering but they are a long way off so good luck to them.

Close to the waterfall the water is hotter, so up to my armpits in Pir Ghaib's sacred water I wash, and shampoo my hair. The sun is above the ravine now, starring alone in a cloudless sky, its rays lighting up the palm fronds. Backing under the waterfall I can rinse my hair under the endless supply of hot water. It's like featuring in one's own shampoo advertisement, the kind where beautiful women with long dark tresses cavort under tropical cascades while a tanned Adonis looks on admiringly from a fern-fringed rock. Well, I've got the tropical cascade, the rest will have to remain a fantasy. Even I can't transform the mangy goat eyeing up my clothes and toiletries into anything desirable.

Down the stream, edged with pink-flowered oleander, go last night's phobias about earthquakes and dacoits – and my shampoo bottle which I've casually flung towards my pile of clothes, missing the bank. No one is at the rest house when I get back but a small girl appears on the verandah as I pack my gear. We play knucklebones with stones. In five minutes she is beating me at everything – horse in the stable, jingles, fly-catching – and has learnt to count the five stones in English. She is about 10 and it is unlikely she's ever been to school or ever will.

I leave Pir Ghaib on foot. I've got over my attack of traveller's jitters and have recovered that knot of anticipation I have almost every day when I'm travelling – the lure of the unknown that becomes an addiction – and I'm not going to let our ute driver demolish it. If he had troubles coming up the steep track, I don't want to be with him while he learns the art of coming down it.

We meet up on the valley floor. Ali and Shahjee are travelling on top of the luggage piled up in the back of the ute. I join them. 'But why?' asks Mujahid. 'You'll get covered in dust.' Because at home we can't legally travel like this any more. We have to be inside with seatbelts fastened. The boys find it amusing that a government should make rules to protect people from themselves. They are incredulous when I tell them it is illegal to ride a bicycle without a helmet. Perhaps this has become one of the intoxications of Pakistan: there may be cultural and religious rules to adhere to but the red tape of bureaucracy stays tangled in the offices rather than wrapping itself around ordinary life.

There'd be no guarantee of safety if I was inside the cab anyway. The seatbelt doesn't work so I've got as much chance of surviving a head-on collision if I'm flung from the ute tray as I have of going through the windscreen. So we hurtle down the Bolan Pass towards the railway station at Mach. I've wound my dupatta around my face to keep out the worst of the dust. Ali and Shahjee wear their scarves Arabian style, tightly wrapped around their heads, leaving a gap just wide enough for sunglasses to poke through. The wind funnelling through the pass is strong and when we hit the inevitable potholes the three of us bounce in unison several centimetres off the packs. Mujahid turns occasionally from his seat alongside the driver and rolls his eyes at me.

He and I are going to travel back to Quetta by train from Mach along one of the most famous stretches of railway line in the world. There obviously haven't been too many foreign visitors recently, though – when I climb down out of the ute in the Mach bazaar and unwind my dupatta the local men (there are no women in sight) look incredulous.

Apart from the railway station and the bazaar, Mach's only claim to fame is a sprawling prison. I don't know what type of prisoner is kept here but it would be hard to imagine anywhere more bleak to be incarcerated. This feels like the Pakistani Wild West although the railway station is definitely reminiscent of the Raj. It was the British who built the railway. The desire to protect their vulnerable western flank overcame the enormous challenge of putting a railway line through one of the most inhospitable regions on the planet.

The Bolan Pass itself exists in the shadow of its more famous neighbour to the north, the Khyber Pass, yet in the past it has been far more strategic. During the second half of the 19th century the British were obsessed with fear of a Russian invasion and the Bolan was seen as one of the most likely routes for a Russian army to make its way out of the mountains and down to the riches of the Indian plains. So the decision was made to put a railway through the pass to provide quicker access for troops bound for Quetta, one of the Raj's most important garrison towns, and strategically placed just to the north of the pass.

Even before the railway was hacked through this appallingly difficult route the British had shed blood here. They'd used the pass to reach Afghanistan during the two Afghan wars of the late 19th century and many lost their lives among the shattered cliffs and ravines, picked off by marauding tribesmen or felled by extremes of temperature and other hazards. Temperatures of more than 54°C have been recorded here in summer and in winter they can plunge to -17°C. There's a local saying that the Baluchis are the only people who wear coats in hell.

It took the British three attempts to put the railway through. During the first attempt those of the thousands of workers who survived the blistering summer heat were struck with cholera. Many died and, ironically, it was the inhospitable surroundings that led to the first line going through – those trying to escape the deadly disease were trapped there and restarted work on the railway. The first route followed the dry river bed. It rarely flooded and when it did the trains ploughed their way through water up to a metre deep. Then, finally, the track was washed away altogether.

Engineer James Ramsay was employed to build the weather-proof 95-kilometre line through the pass that is still in use today.

He did so at a cost of £1.5 million, a colossal sum in today's currency. We're going to take the journey to Quetta, second class, for about $1.70 each. Ramsay's efforts created an awe-inspiring piece of engineering which railway buffs consider almost unsurpassed anywhere in the world. At times the gradient is 1 in 25 as the route climbs from 120 to 1800 metres. There are 20 tunnels and in one 6-kilometre stretch huge steel girder bridges cross the ravine nine times.

We are early, so we find a bench on the platform and in a few minutes every other human being on the station has found us. Even the stationmaster emerges from his office to check me out. A cold wind blows down the platform, picking up pieces of newspaper and tattered plastic bags, but with the semicircle of observers pressed around me I am nicely sheltered. Mujahid answers the gathering's questions about me – where is she from? How old is she? Is she married (and in that case where is her husband and why he is letting her travel alone)? There is only one other woman on the platform. Dressed in a pearl grey burqa, she walks past holding the hand of a small girl wearing a fluorescent pink party frock topped with a fair isle cardigan.

A throaty rumble announces the arrival of the Chiltern Express, 12 carriages being pushed and pulled up the incline by a snorting Australian diesel at each end. In the days of the Raj four engines were used at times to pull the nine-carriage Karachi Mail through the pass. A jagged line of elbows pokes out the open windows of our carriage but once I get in all the male passengers give up gazing at the arid mountains and stare at me instead.

The floor is littered with the creamy white shells of pistachio nuts and the green vinyl seats are filmed with dust. It's been a long time since a sweeper has been through this carriage. We aren't planning to sit down. We stand in the open door and, out of sight of the fasting passengers (it's still Ramazan), eat fresh Iranian dates, spitting the stones out onto the track. We aren't in any real danger of falling out: the trains are labouring up the 1 in 25 gradient now and a walker could easily keep pace with us. But there it is again, that heady feeling of liberation – hanging out the carriage door, spitting date stones onto the ballast and no one to tell us to sit down.

Building the railway might have taken its toll on the workers and they might have been in a hurry to have it completed, but they certainly didn't stint on craftsmanship. Each tunnel entrance is a work of art. The portals built from local stone are topped with miniature battlements and turrets and each still bears the rather poignant name given to it so long ago, such as Mary Jane (after an engineer's wife), Elgin and Windy Corner. On strategic crags overhead are the ruins of small forts used by the British to protect their precious railway from the attentions of sometimes hostile local Baluchi tribesmen. They would have found it easy to hide up there. Above us the rock walls, jagged and scored with fault lines, dwarf the railway line; in places the mountains reach 2500 metres.

Baluchis have a fearsome reputation in battle and many still live by the sword (or more possibly, these days, by the Kalashnikov), but in one of those twists that abound in Pakistan, they are also great poets. As we inch through the ravine I can understand the inspiration for a Baluchi poet who wrote: 'The mountains are the Baluchi's forts; the peaks are better than any army, the lofty heights are our comrades; the pathless gorges our friends.'

The train drivers may not feel quite so friendly today towards the constant hazard of rocks tumbling down onto the line. Earthquakes are an ever-present danger. We cross a bridge just outside Mach which was hit by a massive earthquake in 1931. The bridge, with two 45-metre spans and one of 30 metres, is supported by huge stone piers and abutments. After the quake engineers discovered it was 30 centimetres shorter yet the piers were still vertical and there was hardly a crack to be seen.

It is so steep through this section of the Bolan Pass that 'catch' sidings were built at regular intervals. Trains coming down the pass have to stop at the points here, which are always set towards the siding. Only when the driver has signed a log will the points be switched over. On one occasion an out of control fruit train coming downhill through this section of the gorge flew into the catch siding at about 100 kilometres an hour and shot nearly half a kilometre up a 1 in 8 gradient before coming to a stop.

Maintaining the railway must be a nightmare but it's clear the workers do so with pride. Point junctions are edged with whitewashed boulders, which also mark out paths down to stream beds or small shelters. We stay in the doorway as the diesels snort their way through the tunnels, the noise of their engines reverberating around the rough-hewn walls. The train erupts from tunnels directly beside the road which intertwines with the rail line all the way down to the plains around Quetta.

The very best of Pakistan's famed decorated trucks must surely be in Baluchistan and we are keeping pace with several of them. Maybe it is the arid, colourless tracts of desert that have the locals craving colour: the trucks are shuddering, diesel-spewing, moving art galleries. Every centimetre is covered with paintings of flowers, tigers, forest-clad mountains and lakes, nuclear missiles – whatever takes the specialist truck painters' imaginations. Their biggest single canvas, the back of the truck, is usually devoted to paintings of revered politicians or religious leaders, or sultry black-haired girls with pouting pink lips. The paintings are set off by plentiful use of beaten white metal or chrome which flashes blindingly every time the trucks on the Bolan turn a corner and catch the sun.

Even the windscreens are framed with stickers, fringes of tinsel and, for night travellers' enjoyment, flashing neon lights. Some owners even remove the doors, replacing them with intricately carved wooden ones. Then there are only the multicoloured spinners to add to the wheels and the metres of dangling rattling chains to affix around the base of the chassis.

The trucks' beauty is more than skin deep. Drivers are only too pleased to open the doors of their cabs and show off the bouquets of artificial flowers stuck to the dashboard, the clutch of good luck charms dangling from the rear-vision mirror (a completely redundant piece of equipment in Pakistan) and the highly patterned plastic covered seats. I wave to the men who stand swaying on one of the truck decks. They wave back and the driver sounds the horn which gives a quick burst of 'Never on a Sunday'.

At Kolpur, where the houses are stepped up the hills on either side of the railway line, the train reaches the highest point, 1800 metres. The pass ends here with a flourish and one of the most fanciful of bridges, topped by impressive towers and battlements. Wreathed in a black cloud of pungent diesel our train passes under the bridge and gathers speed. We shoot out onto the plains south of Quetta like a cork popping out of a bottle.

the road to the top of the world

Apricot blossom lies in drifts across the Mir of Hunza's orchard. It covers the grass like a late spring snowfall. The trees are still smothered in white flowers, though, and through the fluttering petals are glimpses of razor-sharp peaks that tower over the Hunza Valley. A small boy with blue eyes is selling last summer's sun-dried apricots from a makeshift table under the trees. Single white petals are caught in his light brown hair. His fruit has been baked hard, but one bite releases the flavour captured during the last short but intense north Pakistan summer.

The orchard lies at the foot of the Baltit Fort, a fortress that was home to the mirs (rulers) of the Hunza Valley for more than 700 years. It almost seems to grow out of a massive rocky promontory that dominates the valley. From the fort's watch-tower the mir's troops could monitor the progress of traders with their lucrative caravans of precious goods following one of the fabled silk routes that linked China with the Indian sub-continent. The route now followed in part by the Karakoram Highway through Northern Pakistan began to come into its own in about AD 200 and was in regular use until the 16th century. Loaded onto the yak and camel caravan trains coming from China were silk, tea, spices, porcelain and other Eastern treasures. When they returned they'd be carrying precious stones, ivory, gold and rare woods.

Living off the land has never been easy here, with the short sweltering summers and bitterly cold winters. So for hundreds of years the Hunzakuts raided the caravans, regarding this as a legitimate source of extra revenue. Sections of the original route used by the traders – and also by Buddhist pilgrims, explorers, and spies who played the Great Game for the Russian and British empires during the 19th century – still exist. The hair-raising track clings to the sides of cliffs, and where rocky bluffs provided no footholds, narrow wooden walkways were cantilevered out over sheer drops. Looking at these one can only imagine the feelings of the traders who had slogged over the fiendishly cold and dangerous mountain passes between China and Hunza only to be met by a horde of entrepreneurial Hunzakuts bent on pillaging their stock.

The accounts of Buddhist pilgrims such as Fa-hsein and Hsuan Tsang, who came this way nearly 1500 years ago, tell of dragons spitting poison, winds, rain, snow and sand; ladders suspended down cliff faces; rope and iron chain bridges across yawning voids along the route. Hsuan Tsang talked of mountain spirits and demons sending in their rage 'all sorts of calamities' and the sky being continually overcast with frozen clouds and whirling snowstorms. 'Anyone who did not follow in the guide's footsteps will have fallen and perished,' he wrote. 'There was not a trace of vegetation, only a mass of crazily piled rock on rock and everywhere slender stone pinnacles looking like a forest of trees without leaves.' Poplars, apricot, apple, cherry, mulberry and walnut trees may now flourish in Hunza but Hsuan Tsang's description of the mountains in this region is as true today as when he saw them in the seventh century.

It doesn't matter how many times I stand in the bazaar at Karimabad and look across the valley at the 7790-metre snowy slab of Rakaposhi or crane my neck to see the slender spire of 6000-metre Bubulimating, or Golden Peak, looming above a fringe of 'lesser' peaks to the west, I'm always rendered speechless – a rare occurrence for me.

This has to be one of the most sublime views on earth, whether it is in spring when the peaks are framed with flowers or when the valley is an inferno of burning autumnal colour. When I die, someone is going to have to lug a portion of my ashes over here and cast half of them into the winds that swirl around the Baltit Fort. (The rest, family please note, are to be let fly into the breeze at the base of the Cathedral Peaks in Passu to the north.) The fort is being restored and I hope that when the work is finished, the carved wooden lintels and beams, silvery with age, will still retain the spirits of the past that seem to linger here.

Fifteen months after September 11, Karimabad has a deserted air. This used to be a major stopping-off point for tourists travelling the Karakoram Highway but Mujahid and I are the only guests in the 50-bed Hunza View Hotel. Almost all the other hotels are closed and the bazaar, usually congested with jeeps, visitors and goods spilling out of the dozens of handicraft shops, is all but empty.

I am a little relieved so many of the shops are closed. The last time I was here I was ashamed to discover that, faced with what seemed to me to be an unfair concentration of good-looking Hunza shopkeepers, my bargaining powers deserted me entirely. I staggered back to the hotel loaded with shawls, wooden spoons and jewellery and was told by Mujahid that from now on I would be kept away from the bazaar in the interests of saving my family from bankruptcy.

He obviously thinks it's fairly safe to take me there this time. We are using a shortcut from the hotel to the bazaar – a near vertical climb that has me making numerous stops to 'admire the view'. One of the few shops open is owned by Waji Ullah Baig and on meeting him I cross my fingers that he will not ask me if I want to buy anything because I know I'll be putty in his hands. Waji also owns hotels and is passionate about improving conditions for the local people and ensuring that Karimabad's future development is planned and environmentally sound.

Antique Kashmiri shawls and rugs hang from the walls of his shop, and strings of natural cut rubies and emeralds from mines in the surrounding mountains glint in display cases. What catches our eye is a newspaper-wrapped parcel sitting on one of the counters. It's about the size of an over-inflated soccer ball. Waji carefully unwraps it and before us is a glorious hunk of icy blue aquamarine crystals encrusted with silvery mica flowers. It has come from a mine just across the valley and its price tag is tens of thousands of dollars.

'She knows about rocks,' Mujahid tells Waji. 'Do you have any more?'

Waji hands me an even larger parcel and lets me unwrap it. Inside is a confection of smoky quartz crystals, shot through with lustrous long needles and with mica flowers clustered around its base. Knowledge long buried in my brain's recesses floods back. 'Dendritic inclusions,' I blurt, pointing at the needles. Waji looks surprised and Mujahid has the expression of a performing seal trainer whose charge has just managed a particularly difficult trick.

A staff member opens a door at the back of the shop to illuminate more of the crystals. Sunlight floods in from a narrow veranda, as the Hunza Valley, with Rakaposhi dominating the skyline, is framed in the doorway.

'Look at it,' Waji says, an outstretched arm indicating the view.

I am. I am.

'So where are all the tourists?' Waji goes on. 'All this beauty and there is no one here. Why?'

Why indeed. Both Waji and Mujahid are educated men who have travelled extensively overseas, so they are well aware that the West perceives Pakistan as permanently dangerous and unstable. But that doesn't make it any easier for them to accept, especially when the reality is often so different from what is portrayed outside their country.

'It's the bloody media, bloody CNN,' Mujahid says.

I point out that this particular representative of the 'bloody media' has ignored a travel advisory to come to Pakistan partly to try to change perceptions, but I know he has a point. Since September 11 Pakistan has been teeming with hundreds of gung-ho journalists and film crews desperate to get into Afghanistan to make their names as war correspondents.

Reinforcing stereotypical images of the country, and beating up the dangers and the tensions in Pakistan, is all part of the game and fills in time while waiting to get over the border.

Across the narrow street that runs the length of the bazaar is Sher Ali's shop which has floor to ceiling shelves bulging with shawls, coats and hats. Sher Ali's father was a master weaver who was awarded one of Pakistan's highest honours for his superb hand-woven woollen products. His son is carrying on the tradition but now has no buyers at all. He is trying to keep his small staff employed but it is becoming increasingly difficult.

We sit on the floor of the open door of his shop and share a chicken curry. I stare just as much as my companions when a tall Western man walks past, accompanied by a blonde in jeans and a blouse. They do a double-take when they see me with my dupatta draped around my head and my right hand poised over the communal plate of rice. They have no sooner passed when a neighbouring shop owner appears to tell us the couple are Americans, a very rare breed in Pakistan these days, and he thinks they are from the US embassy in Islamabad.

As we discuss how Pakistan is going to persuade tourists to return I suggest that it is going to take time. But Sher Ali, Mujahid and the majority of the population of the Hunza region, who now depend at least partly on tourism, and who have extended families to feed and educate, don't have the luxury of being able to wait.

That night as Mujahid and I sit talking very late in my room over a bottle of the locally brewed Hunza water (mulberry brandy) there's a sound like the rumble of an approaching goods train. The room lurches and the wooden furniture creaks. It's an earthquake. Yesterday, and the day before, two earthquakes struck the region around Chilas, to the south-west on the Karakoram Highway, killing at least 11 people and leaving about 4000 homeless. It also closed the highway for days. What we've just experienced is an aftershock.

Above us is a thick concrete beam and two more floors of the hotel. Into my mind flash images of dozens of Reuter photographs I've seen over the years of buildings that have collapsed like packs of cards. 'Do you think we should sleep outside?' I ask Mujahid.

'Why?'

'Because I don't want to be crushed under the top two floors of this hotel,' I tell him.

'And outside the radio mast and the whole hotel can fall on us,' he points out. 'If it is going to happen we may as well be comfortable until then.'

I tell him it could be embarrassing if the hotel is flattened and they pull out two bodies from the same room.

'Especially as this is known as the honeymoon suite,' Mujahid says.

Earthquakes are commonplace along the Karakoram Highway although the present tremors are some of the more deadly in recent years. One estimate is that there's an earthquake every three minutes somewhere along its route. In geological terms, this is one of the most active places in the world. Nanga Parbat, the first of the spectacular peaks that come into view along the highway on the drive north, is growing at about 7 millimetres a year, one of the fastest uplifts on the planet. The reason for all this geological rock and roll lies underground. The three great mountain ranges that converge in this region are the result of probably the largest collision ever to occur on earth – the clash

119

between the Indian and Asian tectonic plates. This created the Himalayan, Karakoram and Hindu Kush ranges.

Some of the most unstable and spectacular stretches of the highway are where the road clings to the walls of the gorge above the Indus River, north of Besham and before one reaches Gilgit. In theory this is a two-lane highway but drivers tend to make use of the whole width of the road. This does have advantages for passengers because no matter which side of the vehicle you are sitting on there is always an unimpeded, gut-wrenching view straight down into the swirling brown waters of the Indus. Transfixed, I spot two people steering a small raft through the turbulent water towards a khaki-coloured tent that has been pitched near the water's edge. A small herd of black and white long-eared goats is scattered over the river bank nearby. This is a home of the semi-nomadic Kohistani gold miners who eke out a living panning for the precious metal along the river. Some still use inflated animal skins to traverse the water.

I can't decide if the drivers are oblivious to the lethal dangers or if knowing about them makes them slightly delirious. We shoot past labouring trucks with our tyres rattling in the few centimetres of gravel between the tarseal and the void, or duel for the lead with other buses as we both close in on hairpin bends above the river.

'I don't really want to end up in the gorge,' I say.

Mujahid waves his hand over the view that fills the bus window – the crags looming over our heads, the Indus boiling and frothing over the boulders below, the snowy bulk of the Nanga Parbat in the distance. 'Would it really be so bad to die here?'

The landscape oozes rawness and instability. Thermal springs bubble right beside the road, the edges of the steaming hot streams encrusted with sulphur crystals. In places the road cuts over vast expanses of scree that stretch thousands of metres from the peaks above into the river. The thin ribbon of tarseal is completely insignificant. Huge boulders sit delicately poised on near vertical mountainsides. In some places the route has been blasted through solid rock, leaving jagged slabs poised dagger-like above the traffic.

It took 15,000 Pakistani soldiers and up to 20,000 Chinese workers about 20 years to complete the full length of the 1200-kilometre Karakoram Highway. It was officially opened in 1982 (tourists were allowed the full length of the KKH for the first time in May 1986). The Pakistanis, with justifiable pride, call it the eighth wonder of the world. More than 800 Pakistanis and 80 Chinese died building the road. At times the workers had to be suspended by ropes along the most inaccessible sections. Many fell to their deaths or were crushed by falling rocks.

On a previous journey I narrowly escaped one of these unguided missiles. We were crossing an unsealed section where, just days earlier, a slip had swept the tarseal into the Indus. The driver slammed on his brakes as a slab of rock detached itself from the shattered cliff on our right and dropped into the middle of the road. 'Allah be thanked,' he said, as a small cloud of dust rose from the debris. Mujahid got out and rolled the slab over the edge. He didn't look overhead. Inshallah, more wouldn't fall but if it did, well, seeing it coming wouldn't make any difference.

Despite its unstable nature the road is used as an extension of people's living space, and in a region where there is so little flat land it is especially useful for games of cricket. There are special challenges when playing on the highway. Stepping back to take a catch can be perilous if you're fielding near the cliff edge and having to relocate makeshift wickets every time a vehicle comes past must be tedious. Losing the ball into the Indus tends to be fairly final as well. But millions of Pakistani men and boys love cricket to the point of obsession so these inconveniences are overlooked. I've seen games being conducted on tiny terraced fields on vertical hillsides and in the cities there are often so many games squeezed onto the one park that outfielders could take catches for several games simultaneously.

Just before Gilgit is a mind-boggling meeting of mountains and rivers. We stop here just as the sun is starting to drop behind the mountains, creating deep shadows in the gorge where the Gilgit and Indus Rivers converge. On the left is the Gilgit, flowing from its source on the watershed between China and Pakistan, and to the right, the Indus snakes down on its journey from Tibet. Immediately behind this tumultuous meeting rise the Karakorams, to the left of this the first ridges of the Hindu Kush stretch round towards Gilgit and on the right is the very last sweep of the Himalayas.

Beyond Karimabad the road heads towards the heart of the Karakorams through what looks like a gloriously chaotic quarry. There are drifts of fine river sand, vast wastelands of gravels and boulders the size of Hunza houses abandoned by glaciers long ago.

The first time I came along this road Mujahid turned to me and said, 'Karimabad is good, but the best is yet to come.' Knowing his home village was ahead of us, I decided to make allowances for a little parochialism. But when we rounded a corner of the road a few hours later I was stunned. Pinnacles of shale and limestone glowing golden in late afternoon sun reared up thousands of metres from the valley floor. The saw-toothed ridges were dusted with snow, which lay thicker in the sharply incised ravines that plunged in near vertical slashes into the Hunza River.

The highest of the peaks along the Cathedral Ridge is 6106-metre Tupodan (Hot Rock in Wakhi) and to its left across the valley is the Batura Glacier, one of the largest in the Karakorams. It reaches almost to the highway just north of Passu village. Mujahid and his family have three small houses in Passu and the Cathedral Peaks dominate the views from all of them. I can't really imagine what it is like to grow up in a setting like this but the people I talk to in Passu say they never stop appreciating its beauty.

On a starry early morning I stand outside one of these houses and clean my teeth as the light of a setting moon picks out the silhouette of the peaks. It seems almost indecent to be doing such a thing in front of such magnificence. But the cloudless sky promises a perfect day for a journey that will finally bring to fruition another of my long-held Pakistani dreams. Mujahid, his wife Naseema and I, with family friend Karim at the wheel, are to drive to the top of the Khunjerab Pass, the highest point on the Karakoram Highway and the border crossing point between Pakistan and China.

First we stop at the family's summer house, which is built on newly developed land to the north of the main Passu village. Mujahid's father Hunar and his mother Roima are living here, although they will soon shift down to the older house for the remainder of the winter. Mujahid needs to collect a sleeping bag to use in the draughty jeep. Even though it will be sunny today he's warning us it will be extremely cold at the pass.

Almost at the front door of the house is the lateral moraine of the Batura Glacier. It forms a wall of gravel to the north and is a daily reminder of the disaster that struck the village in 1974, when glacial floodwaters burst through a temporary dam, sweeping away much of Passu's fertile river flats and obliterating its croplands and orchards. The newly colonised land is evidence of the people's tenacity. Before they could develop fields and orchards in these glacial gravels families such as Hunar's had first to create some topsoil. This was a back-breaking and slow business but now cherry and apricot trees are growing around the house and the windfalls from the ample apple harvest are drying on the roof of the water tank and will be used to feed the family's cows during winter.

Earlier in my stay in Passu, Hunar and I walked down to see the apple orchard that overlooks a bend in the Hunza River. As we crossed the laboriously constructed irrigation channels that bring water kilometres down from the glaciers, I noticed we had almost identical limps. Mine is the result of an arthritic hip and I asked Hunar if he had the same complaint. 'I fell into a crevasse on K2 and injured my knee and my back,' he told me, as he untied the cows to let them drink from the irrigation channel.

Back at his house we sat in the sun on his back doorstep. It was hot and the leaves of the cherry trees in front of us were incandescent in the late afternoon sun. Hunar stuck a cap on my head to keep off the sun and told me about his career as an alpine guide. He has climbed on K2 twice, eight times on Nanga Parbat and guided mountaineers on many other peaks including

Rakaposhi. While we talked, his wife, Roima, appeared with a glass cup full of home-made yoghurt. It was icy cold and delicious. Hunar used his penknife to cut up one of the russet-coloured apples from his orchard for us to eat.

We have more of the apples with us as we head for the Khunjerab Pass. The road curls around the Cathedral Peaks and we stop briefly at Sost, which is sandwiched in a narrow valley – the Karakorams to the right, the Hindu Kush to the left. Sost itself is a shambolic, unprepossessing stretch of shops, tea houses and workshops. There are dozens of men strolling down the street or milling around outside the stores. Everyone is wrapped up in woollen shawls or in jackets and coats that appear to be leftovers from several decades of mountaineering expeditions.

Beyond Sost we stop at a lonely petrol station, still deep in shade although the narrow strip of sky above us is now bright blue. The diesel is pumped by hand down a length of clear plastic hose and Karim heaves the jeep back and forth to make sure the tank is filled to the brim. We pass through Khyber, a village that sees the sun for only four hours a day in winter because of its setting so deep in the mountains.

I've seen a rare piece of graffiti painted on rocks in one of the small settlements. Just the two words: 'No Taliban'. Afghanistan is only about 75 kilometres from here so it is not surprising the Wakhi people in this area have strong feelings about what has been happening over the border. Wakhis, like their Afghan neighbours, are Muslim but their interpretations of the religion are very different, especially if compared with the ultra-conservative regime imposed by the Taliban.

The people of upper Hunza (or Gojal as the locals refer to

the region) are almost 100 per cent Ismaili Muslim. Ismailis are a sect that split from the Shia Muslims in the eighth century after a dispute over the succession of their spiritual leaders or imams that followed the Prophet Mohammed. Ismailis' present imam is His Royal Highness Prince Karim Aga Khan.

Ismailis do not have mosques so there is no call to prayer. When and how often to pray is a matter left to the individual, although officially Ismailis pray three rather than the five times a day practised by other Muslims. Ismailis also do not keep the Ramazan fast, nor is a pilgrimage to Mecca considered as essential as it is to other Muslims. And one of the most obvious differences, at least for visitors, is that women are always unveiled, and relationships between the sexes are much more relaxed and open than elsewhere in Pakistan.

So the people of upper Hunza had every reason to fear any moves by the Taliban to make incursions into their land. People in Gojal tell me they are pleased that the United States and its allies have removed them. But at the same time they resent the subsequent damage they believe Western politicians and media have inflicted on their country's image.

They are very sensitive about this. Mujahid doesn't like me taking photos of any men with bushy beards because he says so many Westerners have become conditioned to wrongly link anyone with untrimmed facial hair with terrorism. 'These men are nothing to do with Osama bin Laden but people will look at them and say "See? The Taliban are everywhere." '

Mujahid has experienced this stereotyping himself. His name, which means Warrior for God, led to his being grilled by a European immigration official. 'It is the name my father gave me, it is not my profession.'

'So, what are the chances of meeting Osama up here?' I ask, as we drive past the signs.

Karim and Mujahid laugh. There are stories circulating in Pakistan that Osama bin Laden is far from being the number one enemy of the US. Instead, he is rumoured to have had plastic surgery and to be living in the States as a reward for destabilising the region and enabling the Americans to get their hands on its oil and gas reserves.

'He is probably playing golf with Bush in Florida,' someone told me.

One tour operator told me that, before September 11, a foreign documentary film crew who were planning a project in Afghanistan had expressed interest in interviewing bin Laden. 'They asked me if I could find him. It was not hard. I found out easily that he was in a hospital in Islamabad having kidney dialysis. If I, one Pakistani man, could discover that, how come the whole of the US military and intelligence forces can't find him now?'

At Dih, Mujahid gets out to show my passport to the men from the Khunjerab Security Force. Their ledger shows I am the only foreigner to have been through here for weeks. Something catches my eye on the river bed behind the check-point. A Bactrian camel is standing there, its long caramel fur rippling in the wind. I push my way through the scrub on the river bank and discover the camel has a companion, a slightly smaller Bactrian with chocolate brown fur. The double humps on each camel are listing gently to port. They are extremely placid and curious and walk slowly towards me, regarding me from under luxuriant eyelashes. The long hair that reaches the camels' knees makes them look as if they are wearing furry knickerbockers.

Now we're following the Khunjerab River through a narrow winding ravine and the temperature has dropped to near freezing. Ice has formed at the water's edge and the rock walls on the southern and shaded side of the gorge are hung with a sparkling curtain of thousands of icicles. The gorge opens up just before a series of hairpin bends that are the final approach to the Khunjerab Pass. Mountains crowd the skyline on all sides and the air is bitingly cold even though we are back in full sun.

At the next checkpoint we pick up a member of the security forces. Because there is so little traffic at this time of year men are not stationed at the border crossing permanently so we have to take him along with us. At the top of the switchback, tawny hills stretch out on either side of the road. Everyone's peering closely at the mountainsides. We're inside the Khunjerab National Park and this is perfect territory for ibex, a large mountain goat. Among the other animals living in the park are the very rare Marco Polo sheep and the elusive snow leopard.

Ibex were once common from Europe through Central Asia, but they are now endangered and this is one of their last strongholds. Karim stops the jeep as our guard points up to the left. Dozens of the animals are grazing on the sparse vegetation. Their brown-grey fur blends perfectly with the mountains, but what stand out when they lift their heads are the males' long horns arching over their backs. These have made ibex a sought-after trophy animal and this threat is exacerbated by the belief, dating back to Roman times, that ibex body parts have miraculous healing properties.

As we climb out of the jeep for a better look we hear the sounds of the first vehicle we've encountered since leaving Sost.

A bus is crawling up the road behind us. As it passes we're greeted by broad smiles and cheers from the passengers, Kashmiri boys on a school trip as a sign in the back of the bus explains. Unfortunately no one can explain to me how they have managed to get from India across one of the most volatile borders in the world. We pass them as the jeep crosses the wide gentle slope that leads to the top of the pass. The mountains here are more rounded and less precipitous than those surrounding Passu. But the heights are deceptive: the pass itself is 4733 metres high and the Pakistanis claim it is the highest sealed pass in the world.

I'm at an altitude 1000 metres higher than the tallest peak back home in New Zealand and when I get out of the jeep at the border my head begins to pound after walking just four paces. But nothing, not even my throbbing temples, can take away from the magnificence of the surroundings. I stand in the centre of an amphitheatre of peaks that, in the thin, icy air, look like two-dimensional cut-outs. A massive glacier flows down from the peaks to the east and beneath the terminal moraine a herd of yaks is grazing. Even Mujahid, who has been here many times before, is impressed. Perfect days like this are as rare as snow leopards.

In the centre of the road concrete pillars mark the boundary between China and Pakistan. Under the green painted flag of Pakistan are the words 'Drive on the Left'. On the Chinese side motorists are reminded to keep to the right. It's just as well traffic is so light up here: the potential for some high-altitude chaos is huge.

Near the border posts is a plaque commemorating the efforts of the Pakistani road engineers and workers. 'This is the story of those intrepid souls who braved the icy coldness, lack of oxygen and the devilish weather to wreak a miracle called the Karakoram Highway.' With an opening like this even the biting wind and my aching head can't stop me reading on. 'It was here that the stony wilderness of Khunjerab heard the mellifluous rasp of spades when the first shovel of earth was laid . . .' Whoever wrote this should be writing film scripts. 'All ranks worked without badges of ranks, suffering the vagaries of freakish weather with a stoic determination, the oxygen-less thin air and blood curdling winds made even a small exertion a fatiguing experience.' I knew where the writer was coming from.

'The Khunjrabees nevertheless trudged along merrily hacking a track in the sombre mountain fastness for the glory of the nation. The temperatures that even in July/August plummeted to -30°C during the night failed to freeze the gusto of the Khunjrabees.' The plaque concludes: 'We are proud of you. Your sons and grandsons will remember you. You have done the most wonderful job in the history of the army.'

We unload a picnic from the jeep and sit on the stunted tawny grass beside a thick sheet of ice. A second herd of yaks, their black and white hair almost brushing the ground, is standing on the frozen bank opposite us. Maybe it's the lack of oxygen, or perhaps the stinging wind down from the glacier, but I suspect it is just being in this utterly beautiful place at the top of the world that's bringing tears to my eyes.

a groom with a view

It was a straightforward email message from Mujahid: 'You have been invited to a wedding in Hunza. Please rearrange your flight to Pakistan because you must be here four days earlier than planned.' As far as Mujahid was concerned small details like seat availability and the fact I now had only 10 days in which to get ready, were immaterial. I was just expected to be able to do it.

Five plane flights, two hours by car, a four-hour bus journey and the grand finale of a two-hour trip along the Karakoram Highway in a packed van driven by a man with a death wish and I've almost achieved it. There's just a series of hair-pin bends on an unsealed road to go and I'll be in Ghulkin, a village at an altitude of about 2500 metres set in a bowl of mountains in Northern Pakistan, only a few hours' drive from the Chinese border.

I think I've been travelling for about two and a half days almost non-stop but after losing seven hours en route I've lost count. It must be extreme tiredness but for some reason Stanley Holloway singing 'Get Me to the Church on Time' has been a constant companion on the journey. After leaving my Timaru home early on a Monday, I'd flown to Bangkok, landing at 4 a.m. and then left for Lahore at 8 p.m. that night. After an hour's break in Lahore, Mujahid and I boarded the night bus for Islamabad where we were taken straight to the airport to catch the dawn flight to Gilgit, the administrative centre for the Northern Areas. Beyond it lies the region of Hunza and the Wakhi people.

It was Wednesday morning by then and I was surprised to be both standing and vaguely coherent. I estimated I'd had three hours' sleep since leaving home. Adrenaline was probably keeping me going – the flight to Gilgit is regarded as one of the world's most exciting and spectacular commercial alpine routes. PIA still use elderly Fokker Friendships for the flights and they can fly only if visibility is near perfect.

The plane was full, although the customary large quota of Westerners was absent, this being not more than a year after September 11. But we did have a Lahore-based film crew on board filming an episode of a long-running Pakistani soap opera. They shot a love scene in the seats immediately behind us between a glamorous if haughty actress and her equally good-looking co-star. Much as we tried not to be distracted from the scenery, it was almost impossible because a cameraman was leaning over Mujahid and a technician was pointing a light directly at us. The equipment looked old enough to have been used for filming *Ben-Hur*.

ABOVE: Take a camera out in the North-West Frontier Province and wait to be mobbed. These Pathan boys are from a village in the Khyber Pass.

RIGHT: Guns and poses in the Khyber Pass. While my Afridi guard has a smoke, I look after his Kalashnikov.

LEFT: Would you buy a second-hand camel from these three? I'm on the camel, with Mujahid Ali Khan and Qudrat Ali Shah (Shahjee) standing in front, ready for a day's trekking in the Sandy Desert of Baluchistan.

BELOW: A photo call in the Baluchistan Desert. Clockwise from Mujahid (sitting in front), Shahjee, Budal Khan (at rear), Ali Nazar, me, Pir Baksh and, holding the camel, his son Qudar Nazar.

RIGHT: Breakfast in Baluchistan. Ali preparing a vast quantity of chapattis to fortify us for a morning's riding.

BELOW: Pir Baksh saddling up 'my' camel. I had all the decorative trimmings but thankfully the carved wooden saddle was well padded with our bedding.

ABOVE: Morning roll call. Our five camels being brought into camp after a night of freedom on the dunes.

LEFT: Open all hours. The security on this Baluchi village store house leaves a bit to be desired.

RIGHT: Fumes spew from a diesel locomotive hauling a train through the final stages of the Bolan Pass at Kolpur.

ABOVE: On shaky ground. This section of the Karakoram Highway, which follows the Indus River, passes through one of the most earthquake-prone areas of Pakistan.

RIGHT TOP: A calming cuppa. Breakfast in Karimabad, the morning after the hotel was given a hefty jolt by an earthquake. In the background are the Karakoram Mountains clad in autumn colours.

RIGHT BOTTOM: The people of upper Hunza have a minimalist approach when it comes to constructing bridges to cross local rivers. While elderly women laden with fodder cross quite unconcernedly, I found the gaping holes in the bridge a bit disconcerting.

ABOVE: A bus labouring up the final incline towards the top of the Khunjerab Pass that links Pakistan with China.

LEFT: Young women in Hunza producing hand-knotted carpets at Karimabad.

RIGHT TOP: This father and daughter on the Khunjerab Highway are heading for market.

RIGHT BOTTOM: Camels grazing on a river bed in the Khunjerab Pass.

ABOVE: Mujahid Ali Khan's family at home in Passu. From left, Mujahid's parents Roima and Hunar Khan, their daughter-in-law Fareeda and her son Ali; a young cousin; Mujahid's daughter Sabrina, his wife Naseema and his sister Najma.

BELOW: The boulder-strewn hillsides of the Indus Valley proved a great challenge during the construction of the Karakoram Highway.

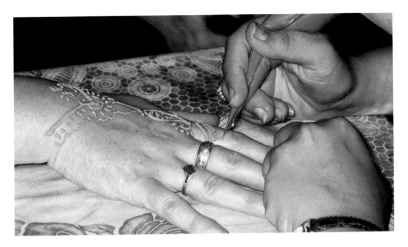

ABOVE: Hands-on experience. My hand is decorated with henna paste in preparation for the wedding of Wafi and Fatima.

RIGHT: A wedding guest wearing a traditional hand-embroidered Hunza hat.

BELOW: Wafi and Fatima in their finery after their wedding ceremony in the jamaat khana. Fatima is still looking a bit apprehensive.

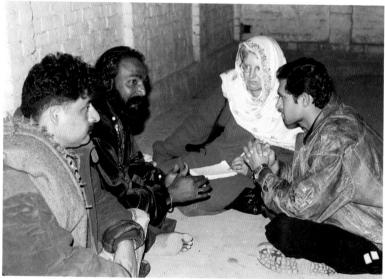

ABOVE: Confection in the desert. The mausoleum of Bibi Jawindi in Uch Sharif is regarded as being a supreme example of blue and white tile work.

BELOW: On the ground. An interview with Sufi drummer Pappu Saien, second from left, with the help of friend and translator Umer, right.

ABOVE: Waiting for rain. An optimistic farmer tilling his arid soil on the edge of the Cholistan Desert.

BELOW: Tea break on the Indus. The long lengths of bamboo at the top of the drift boat are used to guide the vessel. At the far end of the boat Imran Khan is tidying the kitchen area.

LEFT: Standing out in the bazaar. I seem to be attracting a bit of attention during a stroll through the bazaar in Lahore's old walled city.

BELOW LEFT: This classic piece of Moghul decoration is in the Wazir Khan mosque in Lahore.

BELOW RIGHT: Moghul masterpiece: the Badshahi mosque in Lahore. Note the bamboo scaffolding in front of the central archway.

ABOVE: Open plan cooking. Qista bread being baked in a traditional Hunza open fireplace.

LEFT: A Pakistani border guard in full ceremonial dress staring across the frontier into India at Wagah.

BELOW: Flash lorry. This gaudy truck is a supreme example of Pakistan's moveable artworks.

I hadn't realised the action was so close until I heard the whack of the clapper board and turned round to look. The couple had been draped with a tartan rug pulled up to their chins and were gazing longingly into each other's eyes. Surely this wasn't a lower altitude version of the mile-high club? They had to do the scene again because the sudden appearance of the head of a startled Western woman with bloodshot eyes was apparently not what the director wanted for his background.

Out the window the Himalayan mountains stretched far to the east. Snow-clad peaks filled every vista, except directly below us where there were frozen lakes and barren hillsides over which impossibly steep jeep tracks and walking paths could be picked out. As we flew north, the massive bulk of the world's eighth highest mountain, Nanga Parbat, appeared. This 8125-metre peak has a 4500-metre sheer rock face on its southern side and is known, with good reason, as the 'Killer Mountain'. More than 50 mountaineers have died on it, making it one of the world's most dangerous 8000-metre-plus peaks.

Beyond Nanga Parbat the pilot began his descent and we flew into Gilgit.

Now all that could be seen from both sides of the plane were barren mountainsides. As we dipped lower I had my first sight of Hunza in autumn – the narrow valley floor was ablaze with golden poplars and apricot, apple and other fruit trees in glowing red and orange.

The air was sharp and clean, a dramatic contrast to the dusty, polluted air of Lahore and the humid fug that had hung over Bangkok. Outside the airport we found a public van heading up the Karakoram. I was surprised that the driver knew all about the wedding, but I was about to discover almost every person in Hunza seems to be at least distantly related to everyone else.

There were now five of us, including the driver, a friend of his and another guest for the wedding of Wafi Baig and Fatima. I'd met Wafi in Islamabad on my last trip to Pakistan. I had also been introduced to his brother Karim's family who had temporarily left their mountain home in Ghulkin to come to the city because their youngest son needed medical treatment. When I first met two-year-old Mir he'd come out of hospital after major surgery just two days before. His family was required to pay for everything, including Mir's medication.

I had something in common with this little boy from the mountains. We'd both had the same hip operation (I'd had my surgery when I was about four, although I'd had the luxury of several weeks in hospital and my parents had not had to pay a thing). His mother Paree looked exhausted with worry and a little haunted. I discovered later she and Karim had lost an older child to cancer. Mir needed more surgery but the family were now desperately low on funds. When I returned home I couldn't get the Baigs out of my mind so I raised some money to help with the operation. This had been a success and Mir was now walking. This was why Karim and Wafi, when they heard I was coming to Pakistan, invited me to come to the wedding in Ghulkin as a special guest.

The Karakoram Highway descends to river level at Gilgit before climbing again to snake above the narrow gorge of the Gilgit River. It's a tight squeeze at the best of times when you meet an oncoming vehicle, but outside Gilgit it is narrower than ever because of stockpiled sacks of potatoes. Potatoes are a major cash crop here and villagers heap their produce beside the roads while waiting to find trucks to transport it to markets down country. Trees with butter-yellow leaves line many of the roadside settlements and across the river, splashes of autumnal bronzes and russet reds show the locations of small villages clinging to the sides of the gorge.

Our driver is constantly dodging debris that has rolled onto the road, although at times I wish he'd just run over it rather than swerve to within a hair's breadth of the precipitous drop into the river. He also has no hesitation in passing long Chinese-made trucks at the exact moment we are approaching bends with sheer rock faces on the right and nothing but fresh mountain air on the left.

The van is now crammed with people and at the last stop some of the male passengers helped the driver shift all the luggage onto the roof rack. By Western standards we are seriously overloaded, but not here. I can still move all my limbs and no one is actually clinging to the van's exterior. Even so the vehicle's engine labours as we head into what for me will be the final straight. Most of the other passengers are heading further up the Karakoram Highway but must first make the detour uphill to Ghulkin with us.

We snake up the poplar-lined road, then emerge on the edge of a small mountain basin. Directly ahead is a heart-stopping array of spires and crags, including the improbably sharp pinnacle of 7388-metre Ultar Peak. The single-lane road runs between stone walls, some of which form part of houses. The driver, thankfully now forced to slow down, has to do several three-point turns to get around the 90° bends as the road twists around houses and fields.

Most of the houses are sited on the sides of the basin, built on piles of glacial moraine gouged out by the Ghulkin Glacier which flows down on our right. The central flat area is criss-crossed with irrigation channels (most of them dry at this time of year) and border dykes which mark individually owned plots of land. A few black cows are grazing among the stubble of recently harvested corn plots.

The van stops under an ancient walnut. Its trunk was long ago incorporated into the wall around the fields and its branches hang low over the road. Opposite the tree, steps lead up to Karim's house, my home for the next three nights. Outside the house is a narrow terrace and the view from here is unforgettable. The land around the houses is aglow with autumn colour and above this every crevice and every crag of the mountain peaks is sharply delineated in the crystal clear air.

There is no one at home but seconds later we see Karim striding down the lane. He looks flustered. As he bounds up the steps he tells Mujahid he thought we were not arriving until tomorrow. I'm enveloped in a very un-Muslim bear hug and we go inside.

The houses of the Wakhi people are unique. There is always an entranceway – in more modern versions of the traditional design this usually incorporates built-in cupboards – which in turn opens into what is essentially one room. In the centre is the buxari (fireplace) which contains a stove with two separate multipurpose ovens and a single chimney. To the left of this is one of two raised platforms used for sitting during the day and sleeping at night. To the right is another raised reverse L-shaped platform that abuts onto the entranceway partition.

There's a slightly higher platform behind the stove – the domain of the women and used for food preparation. There's a deep step down from this into another work area where a floor to ceiling shelf unit faces into the main room. The shelves display most of the family's crockery and other dishes. To the left and right of this are storage areas hidden from the main living area by partition walls.

The floors and seating areas are covered in a collection of hand-knotted rugs and mats made of yak hair. The quilts and rugs used by the family at night are rolled up against the outside walls. Everyone sleeps in this one room. A skylight or lantern roof lets in light, as does a window over one of the platforms. Windows are a relatively recent addition to Hunza houses. Karim directs me to the spot reserved for guests of honour, on the right-hand side of the fireplace.

Paree, his wife, rushes in, holding Mir's hand. Paree has a flawless complexion with the characteristic pale pink cheeks of people who live at altitude. Her long dark hair has been pulled into a loose pony-tail and she has two strands of freshwater pearls around her neck. She's wearing shalwar kameez but over the top of this has a hand-woven tweed jacket.

She greets me in the traditional Wakhi way: taking my hand she holds it up to her lips and kisses it. I soon learn that the reciprocal greeting is to almost simultaneously kiss her hand. It's a typically Wakhi form of expression, warm and welcoming, and I love putting it into practice.

Mir is watching me from behind her legs, and I can't believe the difference from the last time I saw him. The listless, blank-eyed little boy who couldn't walk has become a cheeky, energetic youngster, who is clearly very mobile, although he rolls his hip a little when climbing up and down the platforms. It's identical to my own gait around Hunza houses. He comes to sit beside me while Paree lights the fire with pieces of twiggy thornbush, puts a saucepan of water on to boil and sprinkles in a handful of mountain thyme or chomoro. This is Hunza tea.

Karim shows me my room, an addition to the traditional house. There are two beds, carpets on the floor and beside it a bathroom with a handbasin, a large metal bucket with an immersion heater and an Eastern-style toilet. The bathroom opens off the entranceway which is the place to leave all footwear that hasn't already been jettisoned on the terrace.

Although it's tempting to collapse on the bed and sleep, it's only about 3 p.m. and there are wedding preparations under way in the village which Karim is keen for me to see. We walk down the lane to what is called Wafi's old house to see the preparation of the special fermented flat wedding bread called qista. This house has the same basic design as Karim's but it is much darker inside. There is no window and no chimney, just a hole in the roof. The wooden beams that support the flat roof are blackened with smoke and the axe marks on the wood indicate that all the timber is hand-hewn.

As I walk through the doorway to the main room, Wafi's father leaps up and pats a handful of flour on my right shoulder. This gesture, a symbol of purification, is extended to anyone entering a house for the first time. Over the next few days almost every piece of clothing I own has flour on it.

Although winter is almost here, it still gets hot through the day, especially on clear days like this. And it's even warmer in this house because there's a massive log of wood blazing in the fireplace. The log is so large that one end is propped up on the sleeping platform and several men are in charge of slowly feeding it into the fire. With no chimney, the room is hazy with smoke. There are about a dozen women at work in here, from elderly grandmothers to young girls, their long hair damp with sweat, faces shiny with perspiration and eyes running from the smoke. Mine stream in sympathy.

I'm immediately given a place to sit beside two women on the left of the fireplace who are rolling out dough into ovals about 50 centimetres long. When the dough is the right thickness it is pricked with the end of a matchstick. I'm allowed to help with this and immediately snap off my match, which amuses everyone. Beside these women two of the younger girls are kneading dough in a wooden trough. They are puffing with the effort and their faces are bright red but they maintain an animated conversation the whole time.

Three more women tend the cooking of the qista. The ovals of dough are slapped onto the inside walls of the fireplace and then, with a long metal spatula, they're flicked out on a wire rack when cooked. The slightly puffy golden breads are then stacked in the corner of the room. There are already dozens of them: the women estimate they've made over 300 in the last three days. Also piled up beside them are layers and layers of chapattis that will have a twofold role in the wedding meals, as edible platters for other food and as part of the actual ceremonial meals.

The older women are wearing gauzy white dupattas over hand-embroidered pillbox hats. These used to be worn more widely but the younger women now favour Western-style headscarves or dupattas. While the women hold sway on two sides of the room, the men have command of the other area, supervising the fire or sitting on the floor talking. Most of the older men are wearing traditional cream Hunza hand-woven woollen hats.

Other villagers are coming and going, delivering supplies or just calling in for a chat. There's an obvious warm sense of community and close family bonds. I'm invited to Wafi's new house. This is only about 20 metres away and is entered through a wall into a garden compound planted with fruit trees. Wafi has spent thousands of rupees on his new house. The room has a window and clear skylight and the timbers are varnished a pale gold so it is airy and light. There is no fireplace but the basic design is the same as the older house, with raised platforms on all sides. Wafi is a carpet dealer based in Islamabad so the floors are covered with Afghan and Bukhara hand-knotted rugs in shades of red. Even the round bolsters I'm given to lean on are covered in carpet fabric.

The massive television set in the partition wall between the living-sleeping space and the kitchen-storage areas is a major departure from tradition. About half a dozen family members and friends (I soon give up trying to differentiate – often good friends are termed sisters, brother, aunts or uncles just to confuse things) are sitting on the floor watching an Indian pop music channel. Shania Twain, wearing a skin-tight black catsuit, appears on screen. In a room full of women whose only exposed skin is their faces, this is ludicrously incongruous. The other arresting feature of the living room is an illuminated picture of a waterfall that emits constant birdsong.

Karim takes me into the storehouse to show me some of the other wedding food. One corner of the room is taken up with a waist-high earthen-walled grain store with a wooden lid. This is already brimful with wheat to last the family through winter. Karim picks up a heavy round object sitting beside the store and unwraps the soft almost papery covering. 'These are walnut leaves and we wrap them around butter then we bury it outside for between two and 10 years.' This butter is then boiled up with fresh butter, mixed with flour and left to solidify. It will later be reconstituted to form bhat, one of the essential foods for the wedding feasts.

We go home, where Paree has cooked me a vegetable curry. A special cloth is spread out by the fire and Karim and I eat together. Paree and the children (Mir, his sister Nergas and brother Jamal) eat on the kitchen platform when we have finished. Sitting in the warmth and quiet of their house, fatigue hits me like a Chinese truck. I've lost track of time but guess it must be late. As I put the light out in my room only a few minutes later I discover it is only 7 p.m.

After a 12-hour sleep and a breakfast of Pakistani omelette (eggs cooked with red onion and tomato), I'm ready for another morning of wedding preparations.

From the first ceremony (usually the initial day of qista making) to the last, weddings take about five days and several weddings, all at different stages, can often be under way in a village at the same time.

First stop today is Wafi's new house, but this time I'm ushered into the separate kitchen at the back which is crammed with women and the bridegroom, who is sitting in the special spot beside the fire. Wafi leaps up to give me his seat and we all play musical rugs trying to find room for everyone. The fire is roaring and I'm immediately handed a cup of chai and a hunk of Hunza bread. For a man who's about to marry a girl he's never even spoken to, Wafi is looking quite relaxed. 'I hope she will like me,' he says. I tell him that she'd be very hard to please if she didn't.

Families choose their children's partners for them. Arranged marriages are still the norm in Pakistan across most ethnic groups and it is often only in the more Westernised, liberal households that the couples get to meet first (in the presence of a chaperone) or even have a chat on the phone. But women and men often point out to me that the West has no right to look down on this practice when such a high proportion of what they term 'love matches' end in divorce.

'I am happy with this system,' one girl at the wedding tells me. 'I know my parents love me and will choose well. Then it is our job to make it work.' A woman I'd met on a previous visit told me it had taken some time for her marriage to work, but she was finally happy. I asked how long it had taken. 'About 26 years,' was the reply.

Mujahid, who I've just found out is the best man or tat, arrives. We do another reshuffle while various elderly women clasp him in fond embraces. He seems to be related to all of them. He explains that as tat he also has a special role to play for the bride. He will be like a second father to her and will be someone she can turn to if she has problems. Wafi and Fatima may never have troubles but some couples do, especially when husbands work away from home (as many Wakhis have done when the tourist industry was thriving) and begin living double lives. Resentments can build up on both sides.

Wafi and Mujahid talk about how businesses have been affected by the collapse of tourism since September 11. Like many other Pakistanis Wafi is not impressed with the way American news networks such as CNN and Fox have, in his opinion, given people wildly distorted ideas about Pakistan and the Muslim faith.

During the height of the military action in Afghanistan when thousands of journalists descended on Pakistan, film crews especially used to make frequent visits to carpet emporia. Some of the dealers decided they were going to get their own back on what they saw as biased coverage and for what they felt was arrogant and ignorant treatment by the visiting media. They sold them grossly inferior carpets at nicely inflated prices.

'Maybe that will teach the one-eyed bastards,' Mujahid says.

Wafi recounts how one BBC correspondent spent $US40,000 on rugs. 'I think maybe they are being paid too much.'

I agree heartily. The average annual income in Pakistan is less than $US400; in the Hunza region it is half that.

I am summoned to the orchard. Three men, helped by a gaggle of small boys, are killing sheep for the wedding day meal. Bloody lumps of meat are loaded onto trays and taken into the house. The mutton will be boiled overnight and served with the qista.

A temporary lull in ceremonies gives Mujahid and me the chance to drive the jeep back down the highway to take photos of the autumn colours around Karimabad. We also have one of his sisters-in-law and her husband with us. The girl cut her finger several days ago and an infection has set in. Her hand is now twice its normal size and she looks very ill, so she is making a four- to five-hour round trip to the clinic. We also have the job of finding the musicians who will play at the wedding dance and bringing them back to Ghulkin. There is not a cloud across the entire Karakoram Range as we drive down to Karimabad. Every tree seems to be on fire.

We find the four musicians and wedge them into the back of the jeep. One is carrying a dadan (a large drum played with a hook), a damal (a smaller drum) and the other two have a tutek (a recorder) and a surnay (oboe). Mujahid asks them to play for us on the way home and a lengthy discussion follows, which necessitates Mujahid rummaging under their feet for a sack.

'They say they will play if we give them some Hunza water. So it is good that I got some today,' he says, taking a bottle out of the sack.

Hunza water is a mulberry brandy also known as arak. A clear liquid, it is now usually distributed in Nestlé mineral water bottles which bear the slogan 'Drink and Live'. Before my last three trips to Pakistan I had never drunk neat spirits but travel in this country where alcohol is officially banned has corrupted me completely. I can drink Hunza water (which does have a slight bouquet of mulberries to offset the robust taste) without falling over after the first glass and can also handle Chinese vodka (peach flavoured is best) and Murree whisky.

But I have drawn the line at the 58 per cent proof Chinese whisky. This should definitely carry a health warning and I can manage it only if it is heavily diluted with lemonade. Even then there is a definite hint of methylated spirits. After my first sip I described it as rocket fuel and the term now seems certain to become part of Wakhi drinks party terminology.

But it's Hunza water we have in the jeep, which is how I come to be holding the sole aluminium mug steady as we wend our way along one of the great engineering feats of the world while Mujahid pours out a generous helping for the musicians. As he hands the cup over he bumps it on the seat back and sloshes me with the contents. 'Sorry, I'm having a blonde moment.' Mujahid, of the jet black hair, now often tells me he is having blonde moments. Another new phrase has entered the vocabulary of the upper Hunza.

Once they've had a gulp each the music starts. The two sets of drums accompany the recorder player who produces a mix of jaunty and haunting tunes as the sun sets and the mountains are silhouetted against a midnight blue sky. It beats the radio cassette player hands down.

That evening I walk across the fields to Fatima the bride's house to attend the preparation ceremony for tomorrow's wedding. The room is packed with people but a space is found for me on the platform beside the elderly women. Fatima arrives, dressed in a white shalwar kameez over which she has a cream Hunza wool jacket. She looks very young and extremely pale. (I find out later she is 18.) She is expected to look sad as this will be her last night in her parents' house.

She sits down on the floor and one of her elderly relatives places a traditional Hunza hat on her head, then drapes a white dupatta over the top. Fatima cries. A tray lined with chapattis is placed in front of us. On top of the bread are almonds, sweets and a pile of chapattis that have been chopped into small pieces. One of the women then sprinkles the chopped bread into a bowl of milk that is also on the tray. We all help ourselves and I notice that one of the elderly women takes extra handfuls of sweets and nuts, rolls up a few of the chapattis and tucks them into a fold of her dupatta. Hunza takeaways.

The next dish to arrive is something I've been secretly dreading – the flour and butter mix. The main component of the dish looks like a cross between porridge and scone dough and it is submerged in melted rancid butter. There is one communal bowl for all the women on the platform but we do have individual spoons. As the special guest I'm asked to go first.

I've never refused to try any food and won't here, but I just know I'm going to have trouble with this one. It's not so much the taste as the texture. And, sure enough, my stomach agrees. I swallow it, just, but it comes straight back up like a parcel in an express lift. Everyone is watching me so I swallow again, trying to hide the convulsions in my throat. This time I succeed. And immediately my neighbour gestures that I should take an even bigger spoonful.

The village lay-priest or mukhi says a prayer for Fatima and thanks Allah for the food. At the end of the prayer everyone says 'Masha Allah' – thanks be to God, as they wipe their hands down over their faces and then turn their palms up. I watch and learn for next time, helped by Wafi's mother, who, every time she sees me, makes me feel increasingly part of the family.

Two of the young women who have been looking after me all evening ask me if they can share the spare bed in my room tonight. There are so many guests staying in their houses there's no room for them. We walk back across the fields arm in arm. En route we stop at Wafi's new house where some of the girls have been warming up tubes of the special henna mix called mendi which they are using to create designs on each other's hands. One of the girls is the acknowledged mendi expert and, in consultation with a friend, draws a design on the inside of my left hand. I have a fern-like pattern along each finger and a swirly paisley spiral on my palm. One of my room mates then whisks me off to the kitchen to apply a sugar and water coating over the design – this, she tells me, will make the final colour much deeper. We then hold our hands over the fire to help the henna paste dry faster.

Back at Karim's house we chip the paste off in the bathroom to reveal a bright orange design. I can still see faint traces of it two weeks later.

It's the wedding day. I put on my new shalwar kameez and some black sandals with heels, even though the terrain around the village is hardly suitable. Last night at Wafi's new house girls from all over the village were calling in to use the iron and there was much discussion about what everyone would be wearing. I am not going to wear my camping sandals on a day like this, even if I break an ankle on the cross-country walk across the fields. I decide it's a day for nail polish and stand out on the terrace to apply it. I immediately find myself painting the nails of every girl who walks past the house.

The day's activities start at Wafi's old house – it's now his turn for the official preparation ceremony. A tray is put in front of him that contains a new white kameez, and a red and white silk turban decorated with pearls. As best man, Mujahid is in charge of placing the turban on Wafi and then sprinkling him with the sweets and nuts that are also on the tray. The mukhi prays the marriage will be a success, that Wafi will look after his bride, that Fatima will obey him and that her in-laws will care for her like a daughter. Then I'm whisked away to the wide street that runs through the village.

The musicians are sitting on a rug that's been placed against a stone wall. Gradually a crowd of several hundred gathers, leaving a rectangular space in front of the musicians. It's an absolutely perfect day – no clouds, no breeze. The jagged spires and crags that lie slightly to the north in the direction of

Mujahid's village of Passu form a backdrop. The musicians start playing. This time the drums accompany a man on the oboe. Small boys lean over the wall giving cheek. One of the drummers suddenly leaps up and the kids disappear, giggling.

Gradually, older men from the audience, all wearing cream Hunza wool hats, stand up and form a line. They begin to dance, slow deliberate steps in a wide circle, their arms outstretched. As the tempo increases they begin to twirl and stamp their feet harder, dipping their shoulders and then raising their arms above their heads.

When they sit down their place is taken by a group of younger men with a following of about six small boys. The smallest child looks only about four but already he can perfectly imitate all the dance steps. My neighbour, an elderly woman, nudges me and points at a tall, clean-shaven handsome dancer in Western clothes: 'My son,' she says proudly. As he dances past us she swivels her hands at her wrists as a sign of respect.

The dance ends and a murmur from the crowd makes us all turn and look down the road. The wedding party is coming. Fatima is wearing a bright red shalwar kameez and dupatta which have been embroidered with gold thread. She has rings on every finger, including one attached by a chain to a thick gold bracelet around her wrist. Her long chestnut hair hangs loose on each side of her face and her forehead is covered with the decorative headdress of metal bells. Wafi walks beside her in his white shalwar kameez over which he wears a black jacket and a thick garland of white tinsel. Next to him walks Mujahid, wearing a black suit.

They have come from the jamaat khana, the local Ismaili Muslims' combined community centre and prayer house, where the wedding ceremony itself has taken place. I realise that, after travelling several thousand kilometres in response to a wedding invitation, I seem to have missed the actual ceremony. Did someone forget to come to find me?

I make discreet enquiries and learn that although, as a non-Muslim, I can go into mosques, I can't enter the jamaat khana (even though in almost every way Ismailis are much more liberal in their beliefs than other Muslims). Inside the couple exchanged rings, shook hands (there is no kissing), listened to the mukhi read from the Koran and confirmed they agreed to the marriage. This was witnessed only by the immediate family and wedding party members such as Mujahid. Although there is no way round this prohibition I suspect the family may have been embarrassed that I could not attend the ceremony. Perhaps they were hoping that, among all the other festivities, I wouldn't notice.

The wedding party sits down on a quilt and the dancing continues. Wafi is talking to Mujahid and other women sitting around Fatima but not to his wife. She meanwhile is keeping her eyes down and still looks a little upset. When Wafi and Mujahid stand up to join the dancing I watch her and note that she's studying her new husband carefully from under her veil.

It may be the tail end of autumn in the Karakorams but the temperature must be over 30°C and I'm feeling the heat. A young woman picks her way across the crowd and leans down in front of me. 'I have a message for you. Please come with me.' Unsure who can possibly be sending me messages when everyone I know is sitting in the circle, I follow. Once away from everyone's gaze she says, 'I thought you looked hot and thirsty. Come to my house for a cup of tea and then you can go back.'

I have a couple of breaks like this during the hours of dancing. Unlike everyone else here, I'm unused to sitting on the ground for such long periods of time so being able to stand up occasionally is a relief. I have the added disadvantage of my arthritic hip which seriously limits the range of positions I can sit in. Although I hope I look younger than the senior women I'm sitting with I certainly don't seem as flexible.

As I head back from my third tea break I'm met by Karim who's been looking for me. It's time to go to the bride's house for the wedding meal. There are dozens of people standing outside the house, and more spilling onto the verandah. I'm ushered into a whitewashed room, one end of which is decorated with gold tinsel. Wafi and Fatima are sitting underneath this. Wafi is the only male in the room apart from a man making the wedding video and his assistant, Karim's 16-year-old nephew Tawakal.

Tawakal is living with Karim's family while he attends school. His village is even more remote and there is no senior high school there. He loves studying science and has made it his mission to teach me Wakhi in two days. At present, though, his job is to stick the two naked wires attached to the lighting equipment into the nearest plug socket. I'm now used to being illuminated like a rabbit caught in the car headlights because I'm always given seats near members of the wedding party. This time I'm next to Wafi.

'How's it going?' I ask.

'Fine, I think,' he says.

'Has Fatima spoken to you yet?'

'No, not yet. Maybe she is not happy with me.'

I tell him that I watched her checking him out during the

dancing and that I was pretty sure she liked what she saw.

The door opens and three men come in bearing platters piled with lumps of mutton. The woman on my left, whose deeply lined face makes her look at least 80 when she is probably only about 60, reaches over and selects the most choice pieces of meat for me. She points to the piles of bread.

'Qista,' I say, or think I say.

She dissolves into fits of giggles and jabs me hard in the ribs and then doubles over again, laughing. What have I said? Something in her manner suggests it wasn't just the wrong word but that I've somehow managed to inadvertently commit some kind of Wakhi impropriety. I look at her quizzically. She forms a circle with forefinger and thumb and, still cackling, jabs her other forefinger through the hole.

Oh God. This may be the first Wakhi wedding in history where penises have been served up with the mutton.

We drink a cup of tea to finish the meal and immediately the last cup is put down, everyone stands up and makes a rush for the door. I'm accustomed to this, as usual by learning by my mistakes. At one of the houses I visited yesterday I was taking my time over my tea, oblivious to the fact that everyone was poised to go. As I swallowed the last mouthful I was almost trampled in the stampede to leave. There are so many houses to visit that everyone has to be on the run from one place to the next.

We are now heading for Wafi's house for another feast. Najma, Mujahid's sister, and one of my favourite people in Hunza, walks with me. She is a gentle person with an engaging smile and after several meetings over the years we seem to have built up a rapport. She explains to me that there are so many meals because the bride's relatives are invited to some and the groom's to others. Because I am a special guest I go to all of them. Another meal of mutton follows and I'm dismayed to find that the old woman with the ribald sense of humour is also related to both bride and groom. She arrives after me and proceeds to tell the whole room about my slip-up.

When the other guests leave I find myself sitting in Wafi's living room with him leaning against one wall, and Fatima and a sister sitting cross-legged opposite him. Mir and another small boy are watching pop videos again. It seems a good time to leave. Everyone looks exhausted but it's only a temporary reprieve for Wafi and Fatima. They still have more duties to perform, taking left-over wedding food around village homes.

One of the most endearing features of Wakhi life is that every home is an open home so I've only been back at Karim's for five minutes when Mujahid arrives, followed by Karim and a steady stream of other village men. Word has spread that I have smuggled red wine into Pakistan. The musicians are supposed to be coming too but sundry children sent to get them can find no trace of them.

When the party moves on to the Chinese whisky I go to bed and wake early next morning to find I have another room mate. Mujahid is sleeping off the effects of the party in the spare bed. He is up before me, none the worse for wear, because he and the wedding party have to visit the bride's house. This is their final check to confirm her family are happy with the marriage and the wedding settlement. There are no dowries here but the groom's family give the bride's family 5000 rupees (about $NZ165) which she keeps either for her own use or for her new family.

We are to leave the village when that visit has finished and drive to Mujahid's village of Passu.

'Be packed by 11 a.m. Make sure you are ready.' From previous experience I know there will be no need to get ready until about 12.30 p.m. so I spend the morning exploring the village. By now I recognise many people by sight and everyone I meet stops to say hello. I come across a venerable walnut tree, the sun filtering through its golden leaves. It is growing in a courtyard of one of the few really old Hunza houses still left in the village. The walls are made of stones and the verandah, which stretches the full length of the front of the house, is supported by intricately carved wooden posts. Through the posts I can see the snow-capped mountains behind the village.

I walk past the tiny bazaar and the women's co-operative shop and climb a hill of glacial moraine to the site of the Aga Khan Model School. The view from here is stupendous. Unfortunately, I'm so busy gaping at the mountains that I drop straight into a drainage channel, scraping off a great chunk of skin from my elbow. Back home, after declining several invitations for tea because I don't want anyone to see my arm streaming with blood, I carry out some emergency first aid, watched by Tawakal, who is showing a tendency, after two days of language lessons, to look at me rather wistfully.

'Mujahid is very late,' he says. He's right, it is now 1 p.m. 'I'm glad he is late, now you will have to stay another day.' Oh dear.

Tawakal, having seen my supply of antiseptic and plasters, takes a shoe off and shows me a dirty, weeping cut on his heel. I have a tendency to pass out even at first aid classes so I'm quite proud that I manage to clean up his foot without fainting.

I'm determined not to be standing around waiting for

Mujahid when he finally shows up. On a previous trip he'd left me in a hotel room for three hours and when he finally arrived I'd gone berserk. It wasn't the fact that he was late but that he'd never considered the possibility of letting me know what was going on. It was the feeling of powerlessness and of being treated like a piece of surplus baggage that had irritated me. But my diatribe had not gone down well, especially as I'd said my piece in front of one of his family.

So I take a book outside and find a flat rock under the walnut tree. Tawakal sits on another rock and watches me. He wants to know what I'm reading. I show him my book about Alexander the Great and tell him that Sikander explored lands not too far from here more than 2000 years ago. It's a glorious afternoon and the sounds of another wedding dance are wafting down from the village polo ground. Groups of girls saunter past, arm in arm. Some are coming home from school, others have been watching the dancing. They stop for a chat, tease Tawakal (who blushes but doesn't budge) and then disappear down the lane.

When the sun begins to set behind the mountains the temperature dives instantly. I move inside and am immediately offered a cup of tea by Paree, who has lit the fire. Mir and I are reading a book together when Nergas runs in. 'Mujahid is coming. Mujahid is coming.' It is 4 p.m. He is only five hours late.

He comes striding into the room, a long black woollen coat slung over his suit. He looks very cheerful. 'I'm a bit late . . . sorry.' If Elton John found that sorry seemed to be the hardest word he would have found a kindred spirit in Mujahid. He's already told me that Pakistani men never apologise so this was a major departure from the norm.

'Are you? I've been so busy I've hardly noticed.'

He scrutinises me for signs of imminent combustion, and can't find any. 'So, what have you been doing?'

I tell him about my day while Tawakal glowers at him from the other side of the room. Then, in as casual a tone as I can manage, I ask him where he's been all day.

'Well, we finished the ceremony at 11 a.m. as I said we would and then someone invited us out for drinks, so we've been at his house up there.' He points out the window to a settlement clinging to a mountain at an altitude of about 3000 metres.

He hoists up my pack and heads outside to the jeep. Another man called Karim is driving and there are three men in the back. I'm astonished to see one of them is Wafi.

When I tease him that it seems very soon to be escaping from married life, he says, 'No, no. Everything is fine but I thought if I was away for a few hours it might give her time to get more used to the idea.' He assures me that Fatima is starting to talk to him and that he is very happy about the wedding.

They've all been on the Chinese whisky but Mujahid assures me Karim has not. I'm relieved because it is now dusk and we have to drive back down the switchback road before heading north on the highway. (Two days later he tells me Karim had drunk just as much as him, but he'd lied in case I'd refused to get in the jeep. Strangely, I hadn't noticed a thing wrong with Karim's driving.) Tawakal meanwhile has wrested the pack from Mujahid and carefully stowed it in the jeep.

Out on the terrace Paree and I hug. Then she undoes one of her strings of pearls and fastens them around my neck before waving me goodbye.

getting high on religion

Don't come to our party without a drum
Stand up and play the melody
I am God
That's all we want to hear
And drink!
Get drunk on the wine that cannot be found even in paradise.
                    Jalaluddin Rumi (Sufi poet 1207–1273)

Thursday nights outside Lahore's Shah Jamal shrine give a whole new meaning to the term traffic jam. We are crammed into a tiny car that is finding it almost impossible to thread through the congested thoroughfares surrounding the shrine. Pedestrians, all men, are heading towards the gateway. They, too, are having trouble finding a path between the horse-drawn carriages, the motorised rickshaws spewing rank diesel fumes and the odd few foolhardy motorists like us. The street is packed and people squeeze so tightly past our car that the panel work is popping. In front of us a driver is attempting to back his horse and carriage, apparently over our bonnet. Beyond him, three men are bodily lifting a rickshaw out of a snarl-up.

Cricket matches and political rallies often attract crowds like this – everyone from rickshaw drivers and students to prosperous businessmen – but tonight the drawcard is religion and the drumming of Sufi, Pappu Saien.

Sufism is the mystic element of Islam that's little understood in the West. Finding Allah or God through love, art and asceticism is a far cry from concepts of Holy War and strict adherence to religious laws. Sufis believe these experiences can lead to trance and revelation and thus provide a path to personal contact with God. Believers are found in Islamic communities all over the globe but it is not an exclusively Muslim concept. One of the greatest Sufi mystics, Ibn Arabi (who died in 1240), used poetry to explain this.

My heart holds within it every form
It contains a pasture for gazelles
A monastery for Christian monks
There is a temple for idol-worshippers
A holy shrine for pilgrims
There is a table of the Torah
and the book of the Koran
I follow the religion of Love
and go whichever way His camel leads me
This is the true faith
This is the true religion.

Pappu Saien has agreed to talk to me before his performance. We meet in a whitewashed brick courtyard that opens off the shrine where Sufi saint Shah Jamal was buried 400 years ago. Pappu is wearing a long black velvet gown, the colour and texture of a Lahore night. He's a tall man, with black hair that curls past his shoulders and a thick, well-trimmed beard. Around his neck are strings of semi-precious stones and several amulets. He also wears several rings, bracelets and anklets. All have significance: the earrings prevent him from listening to anything unkind and the anklets stop him from taking the wrong step. As we sit down a man slips past me and drapes a garland of scarlet rose petals around Pappu's neck.

Pappu is flanked by his drumming partner, Jhura, a younger man with a dapper moustache, and other followers, including a leading Pakistani movie star, Haq Nawaz. Interpreting for me is Umer, a friend from Lahore who regularly attends these Thursday night performances.

Pappu Saien explains that his drumming has a special Sufi beat, a prayer to Shah Jamal which brings him and his listeners closer to God. 'It's a God-given thing – my hands move automatically. I could not beat a set of normal drums. It comes from the soul and because of this every performance will be different.'

A young boy arrives with a tray on which is a china cup of murky-looking tea for Pappu. It doesn't look appetising but does have a distinctive aroma. Umer explains quietly that it's made from marijuana – a kind of supercharged herbal tea. Drugs are illegal in Pakistan but authorities seem to turn a blind eye to the consumption of marijuana or hashish at the shrine during ceremonies. It is used by some devotees to achieve a heightened state of trance. Umer estimates this police tolerance is abused by about a quarter of the audience who are less interested in spiritual enlightenment and more in having a hassle-free smoke.

Pappu drinks his tea and tells me his real name is Zullfikar Ali (Pappu Saien is a term of respect). He is the son of another Sufi drummer, Luddun Saien. His parents had been childless for many years before receiving a revelation they would have a son who would become a drummer. Pappu Saien began studying the art when he was a boy, performing in public when he was 12. As well as playing in front of thousands in Pakistan, he's also drummed in Germany and appeared in many document-aries. 'But it is always an act of devotion, an expression of love for God and for the saints.'

Pappu believes the mysticism of the drums and the dancing that accompanies it is not something revealed only to Muslims. 'It is a God-given act that can affect anyone spiritually. All music will one day finish but this beat will remain. It does not matter if you are not a Muslim, the atmosphere affects everyone. It is a place where people feel themselves becoming closer to God.'

It is time for the drumming to begin. Umer and I find a place in the front row and sit on a thin bamboo mat. The audience is about six deep around the rectangular courtyard and as the performance progresses more people squeeze in against the walls. Balconies and staircases leading into the shrine also fill with people. The more athletic climb into the spreading branches of an ancient mango tree in the corner of the courtyard.

Pappu and Jhura step into the space their helpers have cleared for them. Hung around the drummers' necks are the dhora, cylindrical-shaped drums they play with two different sticks. One is a conventional drumstick, the other is sickle-shaped.

Hanging from the drums are lengths of leather tipped with red and gold tassels. They begin to play. The rhythms build in complexity and the sound reverberates off the shrine walls. Pappu is a study in concentration and yet the drumming seems almost an involuntary outpouring. His mind appears to be far away.

We are sitting so close to him that the drumbeats can be felt as well as heard. The rhythm reaches deep into one's being, mesmerising and probing unlit corners of one's mind – and I haven't even partaken of the small cigarettes being passed down our row. The air is redolent with the sweet smell of the pellets of hashish being burnt and inhaled all around me.

Now the dancers stand up and surround Pappu and Jhura. One of the first on his feet is a young man in a long red satin gown under which are baggy white trousers. Both his legs, from ankles to knees, are encircled with metal bells. He begins to spin, arms outstretched, and the bells jangle, providing a high counterpoint to the thud of the drums. This is the Pakistani Sufis' answer to the whirling dervishes.

More join in, some in white gowns, others in shalwar kameez or Western trousers and shirts. Before each dancer begins he touches the drum as a sign of respect and some place more garlands of roses or orange marigolds around Pappu's neck. They begin to whirl, slowly, meditatively, before suddenly leaping with arms flinging wide and twirling so fast their faces become a blur. Only some of the devotees are allowed to dance. Anyone Pappu Saien considers is not dancing as an act of devotion is guided back to their place among the audience.

Pappu dances too, moving into the centre of the courtyard, his drum circling him at waist level, its tassels airborne. Droplets of sweat fly off him and rose petals drop to the ground. Not once does his drumming falter. Rhythmic phrases are tossed between him and Jhura. The sound surges and retreats, the vibrations bounce inside my head. Although he says he plays as the spirit moves him, intricate and precise musical traditions are being followed. Pauses seem timed carefully to keep the momentum of the drumming.

All around me men are in trances, either from the drumming or with the help of the hashish. Heads shake from side to side; eyes close. Some chant 'Jhoolay lal, jhoolay lal' (a prayer for long life). Meanwhile, vendors pick their way among the faithful selling drinks and deep-fried vermicelli snacks. Above us, beyond the one light bulb and blue haze of hashish smoke, hangs an almost full moon – and the legs of the onlookers who have climbed the mango tree.

I'm trying to remain solely an onlooker but maybe because of the effects of passive smoking I close my eyes just to find out what it feels like. The drumbeat now seems to be coming from within. I can feel myself tipping over an edge into the unknown, and pull back. A thin line of constraint has not been broken, at least not this time.

It is more than two hours since the drumming began. Pappu, Jhura and the dancers are drenched with sweat. Pappu's long hair hangs in damp ringlets around his face. Without warning he stops playing and is immediately swamped by a tide of devotees.

Although Shah Jamal is a spellbinding introduction to Sufism, Multan in the southern Punjab is the place to go to witness the reverence with which many Pakistanis treat their long-dead Sufi saints. And travelling there by road from Lahore is a perfect way to put one in a suitably spiritual frame of mind because the traffic is so horrendous there are almost constant reminders of how little can separate life from death.

For most of the 350-kilometre journey we are an insignificant piece of flotsam in a pulsating unbroken stream of trucks, tankers and buses heading south on the main highway to Pakistan's biggest city, and its only major seaport, Karachi. I distract myself from thoughts of collisions by admiring the highest concentration of Pakistan's unique truck and bus artwork I have ever seen. It strikes me as a contradiction that, having lavished so much attention on them, the owners or their drivers then appear hellbent on destroying them as soon as possible. On our five-hour drive to Multan we pass three recently capsized trucks, so overloaded that an encounter with one of the ubiquitous potholes in the roads simply rolled them over, spilling tonnes of coal, a jumble of timber and a cascade of hazardously mobile potatoes.

No one appears to have been injured in any of these accidents and thankfully none involved a collision with the hundreds of fuel tankers on the road. They are also highly decorative and all bear versions of the 'Highly Inflammable' warning although 'Highly Inflammap' is a popular hybrid. My favourite message on one tanker's rear end was the generous 'Love to All'. Some new Chinese-made long chassis trucks have appeared in recent years and even these have at least a little ornamentation and, in one case, the information that it was a 'Ling Wehicle'.

The decoration may be almost obligatory, but other more conventional fittings and features such as seatbelts, lights and even having the engine running while going downhill seem to be regarded as optional extras. It's a shock for anyone coming from a country where even a malfunctioning brake light is an offence.

Despite the incredible density of traffic on this road buses still pull out into the stream regardless of whether anything is coming and tankers overtake trucks just metres in front of ponderously slow bullock carts that turn out from side roads with no warning. There is no point in being afraid so I concentrate on the kaleidoscope of colour and design, and the vibrancy and vitality of life beside the highway. Small boys dice with death waving flags and begging bowls in risky attempts to solicit donations for mosques, groups of girls in blue shalwar kameez with white dupattas walk to school arm in arm, sometimes turning to look as we pass, and then dragging the hems of their scarves coyly over their mouths. Women crouch beside irrigation channels scrubbing washing and draping the clean clothes on nearby shrubs.

Less photogenic, though, are the thousands of plastic bags that litter roadsides, field and city wastelands. When I first came to Pakistan hot snacks, fruit and vegetables were wrapped up in newspaper, pages from phonebooks or even used exercise books. Sadly, this sensible recycling is not nearly as common now. Thin coloured plastic bags are in vogue and they are swamping the countryside.

With so many long-haul vehicles on the highway, tea shops are a vital part of the roadside scenery. These usually have a long colonnaded frontage and a collection of grubby charpois lined up inside and on the parking area outside. They vary considerably in standards of cleanliness. Some have so many meat and chicken bones in various stages of decay under the string beds that the fly count is astronomical. Chai (tea boiled up with milk and sugar) comes in tiny china cups that sometimes don't bear close scrutiny. Ancient tannin stains and even the outline of a previous drinker's lips on the grubby china turn a simple drink into a potential act of digestive suicide.

Times are changing along this route, however. The tea shops are still in business but they now compete against the burgeoning number of ultra-modern Western-style service stations. But there's still a Pakistani twist to them. Under the signs advertising familiar fuel brand names are lists of facilities: 'Mini-mart, car wash, quick lube, mosque'. I try to imagine my local petrol stations building a small church for passing Christians and fail. I can understand the attraction of a quick prayer stop, however. After seeing the twisted wrecks and burnt-out vehicle bodies, even the most non-religious of travellers must feel the urge to pray for more than a few travelling mercies.

Multan is in the centre of the Punjab's vast cotton-growing area and on first acquaintance is not the most attractive of cities. The streets are congested and the few historical buildings still standing are so thickly festooned with electricity cables that it is almost impossible to detect any of the original features. On the hill above the old town, however, are two shrines that are symphonies of superlative blue and white tilework. This is one place where the lack of overseas tourists is hardly noticeable as this is a place for Pakistani pilgrims who come in a steady flow throughout the year.

Mujahid parks the jeep in the courtyard outside the mausoleum of Sheikh Rukn-i-Alam which is nearly 700 years old. I cover my head with my dupatta, an essential for women visiting mosques and shrines. The second I alight two elderly women beggars bear down on me. They have long straggly grey hair, are almost toothless and both are tottering on walking sticks. But they lack nothing in determination.

Mujahid jokes with them and hands them some small change. 'Old girlfriends,' he says.

'In that case you should carry a health warning.'

'There is a saying that Multan is famous for four things,' he says, as a small boy steers an elderly bent blind man in our direction, 'beggars, heat, dust and graveyards.'

It is also thought to be a city captured by Alexander the Great during his Asian conquests and may have been where he was wounded while leading his troops over the fortified city wall.

The Rukn-i-Alam shrine, more than 30 metres high, is constructed of small red bricks, but the entire structure is decorated with blue and white tiles. The blues are in two shades – turquoise and lapis lazuli – and have been used to create intricate ceramic mosaics. It's a tragedy, then, that neon strip lights have been installed right in the middle of some of the most exquisite panels.

The base of the shrine is octagonal with small curved buttresses on each corner. Above this is another octagonal storey which is a confection of more blue and white ornamentation. This is topped with a whitewashed dome. Scores of pilgrims are sitting on the paving stones outside the doorway to the tomb. There are flower sellers, too, with garlands of roses and posies of marigolds.

I pick my way through the crowd into the interior. More tiles decorate the resting place of the saint known to his followers as the Pillar of the World. His tomb is draped with a golden cloth and surrounded by dozens of pilgrims reaching out to touch the fabric or leaning forward to kiss it. The cloth and floor around it are splashed with the clashing colours of deep red rose petals and orange marigold flowers.

There's a mosque inside the compound and as it is nearing sunset men are arriving direct from work to pray, lining up along mats placed on the flagstones. I'm wondering what their reaction might be to finding a Western woman standing at the back of the prayer area. A middle-aged, clean-shaven man in immaculate trousers approaches and smiles at me. We exchange salaams and he carries on to an empty space on the mat. If there's any anti-Western feeling about I can't detect it.

When we emerge from the shrine there's not a beggar to be seen. They are all lined up at the back of a utility that is parked near the gate. On the deck two men are dropping dollops of dhal and rice into bowls and handing them to those in the queue.

The food is supplied by the wealthy of Multan who believe they will be blessed by the saints for feeding the beggars and other poor pilgrims.

Close by is another shrine which houses the remains of Rukn-i-Alam's father, Baha-ud-Din Zakaria. Sitting cross-legged in the gateway are two musicians, one playing an ancient harmonium and singing popular religious songs called qawwali, and the other accompanying him on double-ended drums called tabala. A section of the courtyard has been roped off and inside the enclosure sparrows are pecking at a generous sprinkling of bird seed. Mujahid, who has climbed over the rope to take photographs, explains it is also part of the Sufi tradition to care for local wildlife. Meanwhile, all the birds have fluttered skywards waiting for him to leave.

An intoxicating aroma of incense fills the interior of the tomb itself but we can't linger to see more. Mujahid has been struck with stomach cramps. I tell him it's supposed to be me who suffers from this complaint but he's in too much pain to appreciate the irony. 'It was those bloody spicy pakoras we ate yesterday,' he says.

I know it's not funny but I can't help being amused by the fact that Wakhis often complain that Punjabi food is too hot and upsets their digestion. Mujahid has been known to boast to mutual friends on the cast-iron condition of my bowels while travelling. I'm never sure whether to be pleased or horrified by this. Although I'm still careful to avoid drinking local water I've come to the conclusion that swallowing vast quantities of green tea and, shamefully, a considerable quantity of neat spirits while I'm in the country must be either killing the bugs or pickling them into insensibility.

He's recovered by the time we travel to Uch Sharif, the final stop on our own pilgrimage to Sufi landmarks. Uch Sharif, which rises from the arid plains of the eastern Punjab, is a jewel in the crown of the Punjab's Sufi heritage. Date palms cluster around the base of a rocky promontory on the top of which is a stunningly beautiful mausoleum, striped with blue and white tiles. But this building hides a heartbreaking secret from first-time visitors.

We pick our way through the grave mounds surrounding the mausoleum of Bibi Jawindi. There are turquoise, lapis and white tiles on the three sides of the octagon and on the four buttresses that can be seen from the roadside. The towers are topped with curls of blue ceramics, like buds just opening into full bloom. I walk through an open archway to see the interior and find . . . nothing. Half the building is missing, swept away by the nearby river hundreds of years ago. Intricate tile mosaics cling to the interior walls still standing but, with edges now exposed to the elements, the building is slowly being eaten away. Fragments of tiles must fall off regularly because many are incorporated into the low earthen marker mounds at the end of some of the graves surrounding the mausoleum.

We have been adopted by two small boys who seem to have ideas of extricating money from us for being 'guides'. They don't seem to realise that Mujahid, Ali our driver and Mohammed our cook are all Pakistanis so they look slightly taken aback when Mujahid addresses them in fluent Punjabi.

Ali, like Mujahid a man from the mountains, is tall with wavy hair and skin paler than mine. The angle of his eyebrows makes him look permanently rather anxious and he's very quiet. But he's not as shy as Mohammed. He's a Balti from Skardu, a village high in the mountainous upper reaches of the Indus Valley. From his almond-shaped eyes and darker skin you can tell the Baltis are related to Tibetans who live not far away over the mountains. He doesn't speak much English but he has a devastating smile. He looks a fresh-faced 16 so I'm taken aback when I find out he's 20, married and has a daughter.

The three of them must appear just as foreign to the children of Uch Sharif as I do, but after getting the brush off from each of them, the kids turn their attentions to me. They pass through the gaping doorway of another ruined mausoleum and as I follow, they look at me expectantly. They tell me this is a tomb. Speaking in Urdu, I tell them I know. I'm not going to be conned into parting with rupees in payment for them stating the obvious. They decide to try chatting up Ali who is keeping a watchful eye on the jeep.

I am trying to absorb the beauty of the tiles when two young girls in dusty shalwar kameez in eye-popping shades of fluorescent green and pink attach themselves to me. 'Anglezi? Anglezi?' I'm always unreasonably irritated at being mistaken for being English. It's not fair of me because I know little girls in this remote desert province can't be expected to even know that New Zealand exists. But I want to be left in peace. Being hassled like this is not as common as it is in India and I've forgotten how irritating it can be. 'Not English, I am from Lahore,' I tell them in what is probably terrible Urdu. They look a little surprised but it buys a few minutes' silence.

Some of the decorative motifs contain Persian script and working at a snail's pace like a child with their first reading book, I make out 'Ye Allah' (a cry to God). The words are repeated over and over, wrapped round the mausoleum's towers like a prayer.

Beyond the narrow wall around the ruins the land drops sharply away towards the river. Two white oxen pull a creaking cart along a track that winds between the date palms. Not one thing in front of me seems linked with the present day. Alexander is supposed to have come here too; he's even said to have renamed the town Alexandria before setting sail down the Indus for home in Macedonia. He never reached it: he died on his way west.

In Multan it was hard to imagine Alexander spurring his troops on as they climbed the city walls. Too much of the 21st century intruded, even if it was only the sight of boys wearing Nike caps playing cricket in the grounds of the Multan Fort.

But in Uch Sharif, surrounded by crumbling ruins and with the only sound the tinkling of goats' bells from the depths of the date groves, I can visualise Alexander here, a visitor like me.

He would have been surrounded by thousands of soldiers and camp followers. It makes my little retinue of scruffy avaricious kids seem a breeze to manage by comparison.

Uch Sharif lies on the edge of the largest desert on the Indian subcontinent. It's known as Cholistan on the Pakistani side of the border and the Thar on the Indian side. The desert is studded with forts and we are only about 50 kilometres from Derawar, one of the best preserved. It seems a pity to drive past it even if there are absolutely no Sufi connections we know of.

The desert is as flat as a paratha beyond Uch Sharif and the walls of the fort are a formidable 30 metres high so it comes into view long before we reach the ramparts themselves. I have a less than perfect view because I'm wedged in the back of the jeep with Mohammed and our luggage. It's pleasantly breezy and there's room to stretch one's legs but the atmosphere is a little tense.

Mohammed is sitting absolutely rigid, knees and elbows pulled in tightly at his sides, trying to avoid any body contact. As we are sharing a space that would make the back seat of a Mini look capacious, this is something of a challenge for him. Every now and then he nods off, starts to lean in my direction, then wakes suddenly in fright.

Mujahid, in the front passenger seat, turns around and asks if I am okay. I tell him I'm fine but I'm not sure about Mohammed. 'Can't you tell him he doesn't have to sit like that?'

Mujahid and Ali laugh. 'That is because I told him as a joke that he was to be very careful not to touch his Auntie,' Mujahid says.

When we reach the village we are immediately flagged down by one of the village elders and invited to stay in the guest house rather than pitching our tents. We've only just unloaded our gear when a man with a large paunch protruding beneath his shalwar kameez appears and signals to Mujahid he wants a word in private. He is the area's security officer, or government spy as Mujahid describes it. He is checking our permits and finding out what we are doing there. Our permit is sitting in an office about 75 kilometres away because we decided it was too much of a detour to pick it up. But Cholistan's answer to 007 seems satisfied and he wanders away.

The fort dwarfs the jumble of village houses at its base. Although it was built in 1733, the exterior walls and 40 curved bastions are almost intact. It looks exactly like a perfect seaside sandcastle. The brickwork of the top third of each bastion is subtly different. The fort may be an uncompromising statement of local military might, but that didn't stop the builders letting their imaginations loose on some decorative flourishes.

Derawar Fort is believed to have been built on the site of an earlier fortress built in the ninth century by an obscure Rajput prince. And, the story goes, he was permitted to use as much land as he could encircle by thongs cut from the hide of a single buffalo. It's 1.5 kilometres around the perimeter of the existing fort so he must have found an enormous buffalo and someone who was a dab hand with a knife.

Derawar is less than 100 kilometres from the sensitive border with India and even though the interior of the fort has fallen into ruin it retains some strategic importance. On the eastern side the sole gateway has been rebuilt in stone. This work was carried out late last century during a spasmodic escalation in the tensions between the fractious neighbours.

There are wide apertures set into the gateway to accommodate more modern weaponry than its original nawab rulers had in mind. But the protection on the double wooden doors alongside them harks back to that era. Lethal-looking metal spikes are studded across their surface. They were designed to stop enemies using war elephants to charge down the doors.

The doors are heavily padlocked. The fortress is still owned by the Abbasis, local nobility who have three palaces nearby, and we do not have permission to go in. The interior is mostly in ruins so I'm not disappointed. I'd rather imagine what it must have been like when the nawabs were in residence. The fort did contain a seraglio, or harem, from which all men other than the nawab were prohibited from ever entering. In 1858 a washerman who'd got lost in the fort complex while returning the laundry accidentally stumbled in on the harem. He was executed on the spot.

Derawar was full of work-related hazards. After one bloody siege, invaders killed all but one of the occupants. The only man they kept alive was the keeper of the vaults. He was the sole person who knew the intricacies of the network of tunnels under the fort and was given a stay of execution until he had passed on all his knowledge. But before he could be dispatched, he hurled himself off the battlements.

The only movement on the top of the fort today is the fluttering of lime green parakeets clinging to the walls.

There's also a local legend that among the tunnels under the fort is one that runs all the way under the border into India and across to the Rajasthani fortress town of Jaisalmer. This has never been found and neither has the treasure that is said to still lie in one of the underground vaults.

The low sand-dunes and piles of rubble at the base of the

fort don't reveal any gems but as we walk through them in the setting sun we find shards of fluted terracotta pottery and fragments of blue tiles. And all the time we are aware of the figure of the security officer who seems to be following us. Because of his bulk he's finding it difficult to stay out of sight behind the low-growing scrub. Night is approaching fast and clouds of dust are hanging over the tracks around the village as animals are brought home. Five women with metal water pots balanced on their heads and babies on their hips glide past us. Mujahid takes their photos and immediately one of the women berates him, waving the sole of her foot at him as a sign of displeasure.

The men around the well are much more enthusiastic about the sight of the camera. They pose patiently among the cattle and goats gathered around a round concrete tank. This is being continuously refilled by a camel-powered bucket brigade. A rope is attached to the camel who's being led away from the well, pulling up a full bucket as it does so. When the rope is at full stretch, a young boy unhooks it while a man at the wellhead tips the water into the tank. The camel is walked back to the well to repeat the process. In the background we notice our 'tail' is still with us. Quite what kind of security risk we pose while taking photos of camels is hard to imagine.

Back at the guest house Mohammed is cooking chicken curry for dinner. The only light comes from the open doorway and a tiny shuttered window. This perfectly frames the small white-washed mosque just a few metres across a lane leading deeper into the village. The mosque is adorned with pink and green painted stripes and flowers. Outside our doorway black goats are herded into an enclosure made of tangled thorn bushes.

Three camels tethered to stakes are stretched out full length asleep nearby.

We've been given four charpois to sleep on, although two are still outside to give Mohammed more working space. A girl of about three with short-cropped hair and gold hoop earrings appears with an armful of block-printed cotton sheets. A man in a tie-dyed turban follows her with four pillows, each covered with a snowy white embroidered pillowcase.

Before dinner I'm taken into the compound behind the guest house to meet the village head man and his family. A series of almost identical rooms open off the central space and he and a gaggle of children take me into each one. Stainless steel jugs and platters and floral dinner sets are propped up on a shelf that runs around the wall of each house. Charpois and tin trunks sit on the floor but there is no sign the rooms are regularly occupied. The women of the house are gathered outside a two-roomed building in the corner of the compound. The head man's mother is sitting cross-legged on a charpoi chanting from a copy of the Koran. A young woman who looks to be in her mid-20s hands me a tiny baby boy. The head man tells me proudly it is his eighth child.

Back at our charpois I report on my visit and how I could not help feeling sorry for the woman.

'They believe many children are a blessing from God,' Mujahid says. 'There is no family planning out here, and no school either, and no medical clinic.'

Mujahid and I eat dinner outside under a full moon. Thorn bushes cast deep long shadows over the rock-hard ground. It's time for a solo trip into the desert. 'Watch out for the jackals,' Mujahid says. I'm not sure whether to believe him but decide not to walk too far, even though the moon has lit up the desert rather too brightly for my liking.

When I return all the charpois are in the house and the gas lamp is silhouetting Mohammed stacking up the dinner plates. The three men are getting ready for bed. It's only about 8 p.m. but I don't suppose there's much on television out here. I suggest to Mujahid that as it is a warm night and there are no mosquitoes we should all sleep outside. 'I'm not sleeping out there with the jackals. They even attack the village dogs!'

Once I'm in my sleeping bag I notice that along the back wall of the house are three sets of triangular ventilation holes, set about 20 centimetres off the ground. 'They look big enough for snakes to come through,' I muse aloud. I'm assured there are no snakes about at this time of year.

Ali puts out the lamp and apart from the odd creak from the charpois all is quiet. Obviously the villagers don't keep late hours either. Then I hear a crunching noise that seems to be coming from under my bed. No one else seems bothered, but after a few minutes of listening to the determined munching, I finally crack.

'It's a cat eating the chicken bones from our dinner,' Mujahid says, in answer to my slightly hysterical query.

The cat's tail brushes along my bare arm and I yelp. Mujahid sighs and leans over to light the lamp. There's a frantic scrambling noise and we're just in time to see a scrawny tortoiseshell cat shooting through one of the ventilation holes.

'Those holes are too low,' Mohammed says sleepily.

The lamp is turned off again.

'I don't think it will come back,' Mujahid says. 'And please don't scream again. It is very hard on the ears.'

'I only squeaked a bit,' I retort. 'You would too if something furry ran along your arm in the dark.'

Putting one's foot in one's mouth doesn't usually survive translation into another language. Unfortunately this heedless comment does. All three of them are now sniggering. Eventually the Wakhi jokes dry up. There is silence.

Unearthly wails begin emanating from under Mujahid's charpoi. The cat, fortified by the bones, has returned with a friend. They now appear to be mating under the bed. Someone throws a shoe at them in the darkness. It hits the metal dinner plates and cutlery with a clatter. The cats depart. Peace descends on the guest house. Then there's a chorus of howling outside. My skin prickles. Jackals.

'I told you there were jackals,' Mujahid says. 'We would never have any sleep out there.'

afloat with imran khan

We've lost the Indus River. Somewhere out in the darkness one of the world's great waterways is flowing through this arid part of the Punjab, but we can't find it. Mujahid has been here before but this is the first time he's tried to find the village beside the Taunsa barrage after dark. In the morning we'll be setting out with some of the villagers to float down the river for two days in one of their traditional fishing boats.

We've been stopping at every small settlement to ask for directions which haven't been entirely helpful. When the jeep stops, men wrapped in shawls loom out of the darkness on the passenger side, and after doing a double-take at seeing me sitting there, respond in a variety of fashions to Mujahid's enquiries. Yes, we are heading in the right direction for the Indus but Taunsa is variously 10 miles away, 100 miles away or, most alarmingly, sometimes they have never even heard of it.

Mujahid is talking about trying to find a short cut which, considering we don't even seem to be able to find the main road, seems a bit reckless. But I've learnt to keep quiet, not an easy feat for a Kiwi woman used to having her own way.

There are four of us in the jeep. Mujahid, me and, wedged in the back with all the camping gear and packs, Ali the official driver (he's never driven this route before so Mujahid is 'showing him the way') and Mohammed our cook. Mohammed started as a dish-washer in restaurants when just 14 and has worked himself up through the ranks to part-time assistant cook in an Islamabad restaurant specialising in Thai and Chinese food.

He hasn't had any work today, however. Between leaving Uch Sharif in mid-morning and now, we've eaten only a few biscuits, tiny bananas and amrud (a green-skinned fruit with a flesh that tastes like feijoas). It's Ramazan and although only Mohammed is keeping the fast the rest of us have effectively been doing so as well. Most restaurants and many of the roadside tea shops are closed and even eating snacks has to be done surreptitiously while on the open road. Although travellers are exempt from the fast it's considered respectful to eat and drink where you cannot be seen.

So, although it looks as though dinner will still be hours away, at least now it's dark we can eat 'legally'. While Mujahid gets directions Ali and Mohammed climb out of the jeep and return with oily paper bags bulging with samosas, traditional snacks for breaking the fast. Once the samosas are devoured we start on peanuts, still in their shells and poured into a bag constructed from a school exercise book.

As Mujahid is driving he expects me to break open the shells for him. 'I'm starving,' he says, impatiently waving an open hand under my face because I've temporarily slowed the shelling operation.

I tell him not to push his luck, but he just grins. It's become a game of his to see how far he can order me around until I snap. So in turn it's become a point of honour for me not to. Serving men first and then eating afterwards, and being at their beck and call is still the norm for millions of women here so I'm always interested to gauge my own reactions to being thrown into this role. I've learnt that it's only when an order is barked at me that I rebel. I can't decide if this is a cause for concern or whether it's simply a case of 'when in Rome . . .'.

The terrain here in the western Punjab is dead flat, which makes it all the more startling when sprawling industrial complexes with towering floodlit chimneys and tall metal superstructures rear up above the scrubby desert vegetation. The lights illuminate the smoke and steam that are belching into the air and the mystery plants are surrounded by high walls topped with broken glass and further protected with barbed wire.

Our headlights finally pick out a small battered metal sign as we come through a settlement of a few shops the size of packing cases and a tea shop lit with one low-voltage bulb: 'Taunsa Barrage'. The lost river has been found. The barrage was constructed across the Indus to both help control flooding and to provide vital irrigation water for the region. The structure includes a bridge, which we cross. The waters of the Indus swirl around the piers, briefly lit by our headlights as we pass. Beyond their reach is an expanse of inky darkness.

Immediately over the bridge we turn left, bouncing and lurching down a track to the village and the home of Talib

Huseein, the man who owns the boat we will use tomorrow. We park beside a high mud wall that encircles one of the houses and immediately children appear from the shadows, running towards us, their shalwars flapping around their ankles and girls arranging their dupattas over their heads in preparation for meeting strangers.

Talib, a heavy-set imposing man, appears and hugs Mujahid. More men appear and a group of teenage boys encircle Mohammed and greet him like a long lost relative. He's cooked on their boats before. Meanwhile, I stand like a spare part accumulating an ever-growing audience of small children. Visitors are not unheard of here. This is a stretch of water known as a prime habitat for the rare Indus River blind dolphin so researchers and tourists used to come quite often. But the ripples of September 11 have reached all the way to Taunsa. Recently few foreigners have come to see the dolphins and to experience the Matwani people's unique form of river travel.

Ali has begun unloading the jeep, handing the gear to kids queuing up to help. Talib is insisting we don't try to set up camp in the dark but instead stay in the house the villagers traditionally set aside for travellers. This is inside a large mud-walled compound entered through a wooden gate. Left of the gate a chest-high walled area encloses the hand-pump and washing area. The house, in the far left-hand corner, has a flat roof and is also made of earth.

It's about four metres square and the ceiling is lined with thin bamboo. There's a double wooden door with a high step and we need to duck carefully under the lintel because it's so low. Opposite the door two shutters have been closed over a small, glassless window. The only fittings in the room are five wooden coat hooks and a single shelf, high on one wall. Sitting on it are a large plastic comb and a photo in a frame.

There are four charpois arranged against the walls and these have been piled with tents, cooking gear and packs. And, when Mohammed gets the gas lamp going I discover, also on the charpois are 13 villagers, from men to toddlers (the women are conspicuously absent) who have stayed on after carrying in the luggage. The four of us squeeze into the gaps.

Talib has said that one of the village women will prepare our dinner so Mohammed has prised the lid off the blue barrel that holds our food supplies and sent half a dozen children off to the cook armed with rice, lentils and onions. While we wait for dinner, sweets, chunnah and biscuits from our barrel are passed around and the village men ply Mujahid with questions. He in turn is asking about the river and checking the boat will be ready.

I'm trying to stay in the shadows and recover from that now familiar feeling of dislocation that hits me when I arrive somewhere new in the dark and am bombarded with the unknown. I feel uncharacteristically withdrawn. I tend to be an organiser rather than one of the organised so I also find it hard to cope with feeling powerless when people are making decisions for me.

When Mujahid told me we were staying in a village house and was that all right, I hesitated briefly, not having any idea what that might entail. 'Okay, I see you're not happy, we'll put up your tent.' I told him to knock it off, slow down and give me a few minutes to get my bearings. We then had a brief conversational digression while I explained 'knock it off'.

The children return with our dinner. One carries a stainless steel platter of rice and a bowl of dhal (lentil curry). The other has a lidded woven basket containing freshly made, hot chapattis. Mujahid, who until now has been lounging on his charpoi like a Roman senator, sits up and makes room for Ali and me. Mohammed upturns a saucepan and sits on it. We eat from the one dish, steadily and silently consuming a mountain of rice over which Mujahid pours the runny dhal.

Eating neatly, more or less, with my right hand, is a skill I've practised hard since my first visit to Pakistan. Just as well, because the gaze of all our guests is mostly riveted on me. The only sounds inside the house are the hissing of the lamp and the children whispering. I'm probably getting their equivalent of a judge's scorecard for my eating techniques. I can hear the roar of the river flowing through the open barrage gates.

Talib's daughter, who looks about 10, has been checking me out ever since we arrived. Her gold nose stud flashes in the lamplight as she follows my every moment. She has shoulder-length black hair and her shoulder blades jut out from the thin brown shalwar kameez she is wearing. Although some of the villagers speak at least a little Urdu most speak a hybrid of Punjabi and Sindhi called Seraiki. My Urdu is extremely basic and my Punjabi and Sindhi non-existent, so I'm completely out of my conversational depth here. But, when I smile at her and then pat the space on the charpoi beside me, she comes straight over and immediately snuggles up. Already life will be hard work for her and there is probably little time for cuddles. She has a younger toddler brother to look after and the next day Talib brings his three-week-old baby son to visit us and later hands him to his daughter to care for.

She and I are limited to exchanging our names, and I curse

inwardly that I struggle so badly to learn languages if I can't see words and phrases written down. It's doubly frustrating when you are in the company of people who seem able to assimilate words from other languages as easily as breathing. I find it almost impossible to pronounce her name, which is a minefield of aspirants and consonants. When I try to replicate them I sound like I'm gargling and the other children giggle. I settle for calling her 'chota bahin', which in Urdu (or my mangled version of it) is little sister.

Sitting with her in the crook of my arm I begin to lose that sense of being an onlooker. She's so relaxed, which I find inexplicably touching, and shooting what looks like triumphant glances at the boys nearby. While everyone's expressing admiration that her father has seven sons (and making ribald jokes about this apparent indication of his virility) she's the one sitting next to that now rare species, a foreign tourist.

I do manage to successfully communicate to her that I like her nose stud. Mujahid, who always seems to keep half an ear on my conversational attempts if only to tell me how badly I'm doing, calls across the room that he's sure my new sister would be able to find a needle and pierce my nostril so I could have one too. Although I balk at the thought of what visiting the Taunsa piercing parlour might involve I have already considered a nose stud. But I've concluded I might be 20 years too late and suspect my teenage daughter might disown me if I did. Already my weakness for Punjabi and Urdu pop music, a wardrobe full of shalwar kameez and shawls and my fondness for fake fur animal slippers, give her cause for concern.

When my little sister isn't scrutinising my hair, face and hands (I'm almost ashamed that my hands look younger than hers, which are dry and lined), she and everyone else in the room have their attention fixed on Mujahid. I've seen this happen before but it always intrigues me. He's met most of these people only minutes before, ethnically and linguistically they are completely different, but he's instantly forged a rapport. Everyone laughs at his jokes, teenagers are fighting over who takes a mug of water to him (when in true Mujahid style he simply points at the water jug) and he reaches out and hugs a small boy who has been edging down the charpoi towards him.

Like me, Mujahid lives for travel and travels to live, but we both miss our families. Guilt about leaving them fights with the thirst to see what's round the next corner. Contact with other children is both a painful reminder of how far away his kids and mine are, but it is also a comfort.

After dinner, Mujahid announces he's tired: would I get off his charpoi so he can sleep? This is fine with me, except that since I left my bed it has filled up with newcomers, who appear to be waiting to see me tucked in for the night as well. Before Mujahid drifts off, which he can do with remarkable speed, I ask him if he would mind suggesting it is time for our visitors to leave. They do. Now there's just the question of toilet arrangements. 'Inside the compound, outside the walls, in the river – wherever,' says Mujahid, waving vaguely in the direction of the door. I can't find my torch in the dim light so have to pick my way across to the gate in the compound wall in the pitch black. I can hear voices but can't see anyone so I'm hoping they can't see me. I've no intention of walking far.

Loud whispering wakes me before dawn. Through the cracks in the door I see movement – some children are back already, obviously ready to watch us eat breakfast. Unusually for

November, it is raining. I know this is the best time for me to disappear into the trees without attracting a crowd but I'm warm and the charpoi is comfortable. I decide to have another 10 minutes in bed, by which time the kids should also have got bored and gone away.

Forty-five minutes later I wake up to find it's broad daylight. My room mates are still asleep. Annoyed that I've overslept I step out the gate and am not really surprised that I have a following of children. I'm hoping they'll soon get the hint that this is one outing I'd like to make alone. But no. So I trail around the outskirts of the village, finally give them the slip behind a crumbling wall – and meet two men approaching from the other direction.

Back home Mujahid stirs as I rattle the chain while closing the wooden doors. I explain my little problem and surprisingly he offers to come with me and act as lookout. 'First, wake up Mohammed – he needs to start on breakfast.'

Mohammed has been woken once already. I was vaguely aware around 3.30 a.m. that someone had arrived to invite him to the pre-dawn Ramazan meal, seri. I shake him gently – nothing. Harder – he doesn't stir.

'What! Is he dead?' Mujahid asks. 'Try his foot.'

I suspect Mohammed may not appreciate having me reach under the sleeping bag he's spread out over him, but I do as I'm told. Mohammed sits bolt upright and blushes. Instructions are given for breakfast and we set off. 'The things I do,' Mujahid says, as we head for the river bank.

An hour later I'm back at the water's edge, hand in hand with my little sister, who carries my camera bag like a trophy. To our left the Indus pours through the barrage and the steely grey water stretches several hundred metres from the bank near us to the far side. We are actually standing on the bank of an overflow channel of water from behind the barrage. Constrained in a relatively narrow channel it's flowing fast and every few seconds there's a splash as slabs of sand bank plop into the water.

In front of us is the boat, or bedhi in Seraiki. It is about 6 metres long with a beam of about 2.5 metres. Geometric designs in red, green, yellow and black have been painted on the hull. The upswept prow curves down to the deck space which is covered with mats of split bamboo. In the stern is a cabin, also decorated with coloured designs and reached by a small hatch. The roof of this forms the steeply pitched rear upper deck space across which stretches a double length of rope attached to two long blue-painted poles which are fastened by more ropes to the rudder. A bright blue wooden frame with a roof provides a covering over the aft deck space and a place to rest three 4-metre-long bamboo poles.

There are no sails and no oars – when I was told we'd be drift camping it was entirely accurate. With no means of propulsion at all we'll be completely dependent on the river's current. To get the boat home again the crew will simply drag it upstream, a journey that will take twice as long.

The camping gear has been stowed away in the cabin and Mohammed begins to arrange his kitchen in the front deck space. A charpoi is installed in the space outside the cabin. We say goodbye to Ali who will drive the jeep to meet us downstream in two days, and to Talib and his younger children.

There are eight of us aboard: me, Mujahid and Mohammed, and five of Talib's sons – Liaquat, who is wrapped in a blue and red Sindhi shawl; Javeed in a bright orange quilted jacket and gold lamé cap; Nadeem in a pink sweatshirt; Inham swathed in a green shawl; and, sporting a part-angora Laura Ashley cardigan, Imran Khan. He is about 14 years old but looks about 10. He is confident, vocal and more than capable of standing up to his brothers when they tease him. He also has an infectious, high-pitched giggle. Liaquat is the oldest and most serious of the boys and seems the least comfortable around me. The other four have smiles that will soon be causing havoc among the village women, if they aren't already.

Talib pulls from the sand the wooden stake holding the bow rope and we begin to drift backwards down the channel to the Indus. Nadeem and Inham reach up for a bamboo pole each, and both take up positions on the same side of the boat, standing on the wide ledge that runs from aft to stern. They begin to turn us by digging the poles into the river bed near the prow, then walking back down the boat, leaving the poles where they are but maintaining leverage by moving their hands down the poles. Slowly we swing around, helped by Imran who is sitting cross-legged on the stern deck, turning the rudder by pulling the ropes with his toes. They complete the manoeuvre as the current sweeps us out into the Indus.

We are now floating gently down one of the world's largest rivers. Mohammed is rinsing stainless steel mugs in water that probably began its 3000-kilometre journey to the Arabian Sea, in Tibet. It is laden with silt, and visibility in the water is almost nil. Mohammed has a saucepan of water boiling on a gas ring set just centimetres from the wooden edge of the front deck. He hands us mugs of green tea and I wonder aloud if and when we'll be lucky enough to see one of the dolphins, one of the world's most endangered marine mammals.

Almost on cue, a shout from Javeed brings us all to the upstream side of the boat (we are floating sideways at the time). He's pointing to a spot about 25 metres away. Thirty seconds pass, then a minute, and finally a dark shape arcs across the water and disappears. 'Bhulen!' the boys shout, the local word for dolphin. We've been on the river less than 10 minutes. As we are moving so slowly the dolphin, or possibly there are two of them, stay in view for some time. Our crew, who must have seen this hundreds of times, seem just as fascinated and excited as I am.

There may be fewer than 1000 *Platanista minor* left in the Indus River but this is perhaps double the number recorded during the 1970s before the Pakistani government gave the animal full protection. The dolphin, one of the world's few freshwater species, was heading for extinction because of disruption of river flow through the construction of barrages such as the Taunsa, pollution and frequent drownings in fishermen's nets. Stories that the dolphin blubber was said to cure almost any disease also created a demand for the mammal itself.

But thanks to the creation of river sanctuaries and the work of conservation groups in educating fishermen about the dolphins, numbers are growing again. Boat owners have been encouraged to start offering river safaris as an alternative income earner to over-fishing, which depleted the dolphins' food supply and increased the chances of them being drowned in nets.

Although termed blind because they have no lenses in their eyes, the dolphins can detect light but they rely mostly on a highly sophisticated echo location system to find their food (fish and crustaceans). They also swim on their side so that one flipper stays in contact with the river bed. When one of the mammals surfaces closer to the boat we can see it's a pale grey-brown with a prominent bulge (the dolphin's echo location device) over its long beak. It has no dorsal fin, just a prominent ridge instead. Females, which grow larger than the males, can reach up to 2 metres in length.

The current takes us close to the far bank, so Nadeem and Inham use the bamboo poles to fend us off. Nothing happens fast, and no one raises their voice, until Imran Khan is teased that he's too small to handle the pole properly and flies into a short-lived rage. Mujahid cuffs him lightly around the head and the boy dissolves into giggles.

It's a rare cloudy day and downstream the grey sky and the silty river are separated by the faintest black line of distant river bank. Beyond the steep sand banks there is nothing to see on the eastern shores, to the west is a range of smoky blue hills. The boat begins to turn a circle as we drift into midstream, doing a slow waltz down the Indus. Knowing the exact time seems to have no relevance so I've taken my watch off. I have no idea how long has passed before we see another boat. Unlike our craft its wood is unpainted and has weathered silver. It's tied up beside a hut with a curved roof of plaited branches. The ends of two charpois can be seen in the opening but there's no sign of life. This is a fisherman's home.

Although the river is still fished, water levels are low at present and catches are down. The boys tell us that when they go fishing they'd expect to catch between 140 and 150 kilograms of fish on a successful two-day trip. They fish in daylight but sometimes use set nets at night. They can list about 10 different species they catch and sell, including one called Mujahid.

'That one would be very good eating,' its namesake says.

Mohammed and Nadeem crouch in the bow making chapattis, talking quietly as the pile of bread builds up. Behind me Imran Khan is humming to himself as he tends the rudder ropes; two other brothers are sitting behind him. Mujahid, who's feeling the cold, is curled up on the charpoi under his sleeping bag. Javeed has climbed on the roof over the cooking area and is praying. The quiet slap of his bare feet on the thin wood is echoed by the sound of Mohammed dropping chapattis onto the smoking hot metal plate attached to the gas bottle.

I eat lunch perched on the cross-beam attached to the rudder. It's the highest part of the boat (apart from Javeed's prayer platform) and from here I can see palm trees dotted around villages set a safe distance from the river's edge. There is nothing in the scene before me to denote which century we're in.

Alexander the Great sailed down this river (coming under attack from settlers) in the fourth century BC. Some locals say the design of the boat we're drifting on is modelled on the ones he used to move his army downstream. He was a relative latecomer. The oldest of the Indus River's great civilisations is thought to date back to about 3000 BC.

Between 1900 and 600 BC the cities of the Indus were at the height of their powers. Their citizens made bricks, painted pottery, worked copper, sculpted and used a non-alphabetic script that no modern-day expert can decipher. The cities had effective water and drainage systems and carefully monitored weights and measures but, intriguingly, archaeologists have found no signs of palaces, temples or any indication of military power. Maybe the Indus River was enough for them. Although its spiritual significance tends to be overshadowed by the

Ganges, the Indus, too, is far more than just a river to the people who have lived beside it for so long. The river is a symbol of God and important deities are believed to inhabit its headwaters.

Ahead of us a boat ferries passengers across the river. It's the same shape as ours but has no above deck framework and its ancient timbers blend in with the colour of the sky and river sand. The two men in white shalwar kameez who are poling it across have long white beards and thin turbans wrapped around their heads. Their passengers sit silent, watchful as we float past.

'I won't be an old man like that,' Mujahid says, watching them. 'I'm going to die soon.'

I joke that he will leave dozens of women in despair, but he's being serious.

'It's good to die. I have seen many people die.'

We discuss death as we float on the river that for thousands of years has brought life to an arid land. I feel I'm part of the river. Because our boat is moving at exactly the same speed as the river we create no bow waves and no wake. Whirlpools a metre across form, spiral lazily, then drown themselves in the depths; deep gurglings accompany bubbling upwellings and in the distance a dolphin surfaces. A Sufi poet from long ago wrote a poem about the Indus.

As many mouths the Indus may have
The current is equally strong everywhere
The country is all the same
When you look at it you will find peace for yourself.

Although it's still overcast the day has warmed up and Javeed, Nadeem and Imran have crawled into the cabin and gone to sleep. Nearby, Mujahid is also asleep . . . again. I climb into the prow, lean against the small posts used to tie up the bow rope and gaze back down the boat to the river. My eyelids droop but I feel more mesmerised than sleepy.

The current takes us close to the eastern bank on which tall grasses studded with spindly trees have found a home. There's a tuneful clanking sound from the trees. Half a dozen cows, with metal bells around their necks, poke their heads through the grass to watch us go by. The chiming of the bells accompanies us until it is drowned out by a burst of Punjabi pop music from a village in nearby tall eucalyptus.

A tractor works nearby too and the drone of the engine wakes all the sleepers. Mujahid and Liaquat are discussing the best place to stop for the night. This is more complicated than it sounds because Mujahid wants to find a spot where he can photograph the boat backlit against the rising sun in the morning. Mohammed begins cooking pakoras. He and Javeed have been keeping the fast and this will be their first food for the day, but we are all watching the pile of crispy golden vegetables as it grows beside the frying pan. Javeed consults his pocket-sized Ramazan timetable and then checks his watch. Seven minutes to go. We divide our time between watching the sun disappear behind the trees to the west, and looking at Javeed's watch. Finally the day's fast is over. Javeed turns his palms skyward and prays, then offers me the dish of pakoras first. I hand them back to him. Once he has worked his way through a handful we all follow.

There's a sudden burst of activity as a suitable mooring place is seen. It's an island, dead flat and tapering at both ends to a curved hook of sand. The three youngest boys use the poles to turn us upstream on the eastern side. They chat companionably while they skilfully propel us up the channel, still munching pakoras as they do so. Liaquat drops a heavy length of chain overboard. There's no anchor on the end but its weight slows us down and helps bring us to rest by a tiny bay on the southernmost tip. This will be our campsite.

Mohammed will sleep aboard with the brothers. Mujahid and I, with the enthusiastic if less than skilled help of the boys, put our tents up about 50 metres away. It's almost dark by the time we finish and Imran staggers over the sand with the gas lamp, putting it down outside Mujahid's tent. We drag out a sleeping mat and sit drinking green tea. Nadeem and Inham walk past and disappear from view, returning 15 minutes later with armfuls of firewood that they drop between our tents.

It's pitch black when Mohammed, accompanied by two of the boys, appears carrying dishes of dhal and rice. They leave us to eat then return to the boat where we can see them, lit by torchlight, gathered in a circle around another platter of food. When we've all finished eating, Javeed and Imran light the bonfire. Imran teases me by leaping through the flames, the tail of his kameez just centimetres from the fire as he goes to find the others. We sit in a circle in the sand around the fire, Liaquat reaches out with a sandal-clad foot and pushes a log further into the flames.

Nadeem and Inham each place aluminium pot lids on the sand in front of them. They have a brief discussion and then slap out a rhythm on the lids. Nadeem begins to sing with a clear tenor voice. The song sounds sad and at the end I ask Mujahid to translate. 'It's a song about a boy who is asking his girl why she did not come to meet him last night. She tells him that her brother came to see her so she could not come.' Other songs follow. 'More tales that end in tears,' Mujahid explains.

Then Nadeem starts a one-man dialogue that is clearly supposed to be between two people. The conversation is tossed back and forth until suddenly Nadeem bursts into song. He explains that it is the story of two lovers who cannot find anywhere to be alone. So they hold a coded discussion about mangoes until everyone else leaves. Javeed, who has probably the best voice of all, sings unaccompanied a beautiful song about pride in Pakistan. The flames have died and there is only a circle of glowing embers as we head for bed.

I must have slept well on my thin mattress on the sand because I don't wake until dawn when a voice says, 'Coffee time', and Mujahid's hand appears through the tent flap to give me a hot drink. Without getting out of my sleeping bag I unzip the flap properly and look out. A mist the colour of mother-of-pearl is floating above the river. Javeed is standing waist deep in the water of the little inlet, bathing, and his splashing is the only sound. The island, too, is swimming in mist and my first un-romantic thought is that this will make my morning expedition much easier – there is no cover on the island but the mist will do just fine.

The sun is a deep red ball being drawn through the mist and when it finally rises above it, a golden column of light appears and extends across the river directly to the boat. A dolphin surfaces exactly in the middle of the molten gold water. I can't believe my eyes and call to Mujahid who's closer to the boat taking photos. The boys turn too and we stand transfixed as the dolphin does several more languid rolls in the shaft of liquid light.

As soon as the tents are down, the mooring stake is pulled from the sand, the chain is hauled aboard and we move away from our island. Mohammed serves up thick porridge which we cover with honey and cream.

We're now drifting past fields of cotton. It's noisier here because tractors have been rigged as makeshift irrigation pumps and their engine noise can be heard for kilometres in all directions. At each tractor, either slumped in the seat or lying on a charpoi, is a man, on hand in case of breakdowns. The fields are a haze of white fluff. Women, their heads covered in fluorescent pink, orange and green dupattas, are picking the buds. The river widens again and sand bars and islands appear, giving the boys more work to do as they choose the deepest channel and then have to turn the boat towards it.

We pass a man, stripped to the waist, his white dhoti still dripping with water and his skin gleaming in the sun. Under his arm is an inflated animal skin (from either a goat or a sheep) that he's used as a flotation device to help him swim across the river. He appears to have nothing else with him and I try to imagine why he'd be going to all this trouble. Not only are the river's many channels very wide here, but the journey would also involve kilometres of walking just to cross the river beds on each side.

This area is an ideal habitat for waterfowl, but it's not bird watching that Liaquat has in mind when he disappears into the cabin and emerges with a shotgun. We then stop briefly beside a stretch of river bank so that he can pick branches of some of the low-growing shrubs that are clinging to the sand. The gun, made in the Punjab, is known as a burra (big) bore but that's where any resemblance to conventional hunting techniques ends. When Liaquat has loaded the gun (and he doesn't take any extra ammunition), he places it on a small triangular-shaped wooden platform or tole which he has camouflaged with branches.

A flock of several hundred ducks is spotted and Javeed drops the chain overboard while we are still about 500 metres away. Liaquat then removes his shirt, rolls up his loose trouser legs and drops into the knee-deep water. The platform is passed down to him and he pushes it away into deeper water, where he begins to swim towards the ducks.

The rest of us find the best vantage points on the boat and watch as he glides ever closer to the unsuspecting ducks. Beyond them we can see smoke rising from a hut half hidden by tall grasses. Two men in white have just emerged from the grass and are walking along the river bank in the direction of the ducks and Liaquat.

The air of anticipation on the boat seems to have become rather tense. Javeed explains that it is just possible the ducks are here in such numbers because a landowner has paid people to feed them so he can hunt them whenever he wishes. And landowners take a dim view of people swimming up and shooting what are literally sitting ducks, fed at their own expense.

It's hard to see Liaquat now as he's swum between two small islands. We have no idea if he's seen the two men on the bank. Then a single shot booms out across the river and a dark cloud of ducks flaps skywards. Liaquat leaps up and begins running through the shallow water. We see him stoop a couple of times. He's seen the men now and is waving at us to move the boat closer. For the first time on our journey the boys are using the bamboo poles simply to propel the boat forward. Looking like a misshapen and rather portly gondola, the boat glides towards Liaquat who meanwhile is striding through the water pushing the tole in front of him.

His brothers help him on board and he drops three wet and bloody ducks on the stern deck. He's telling the boys to move the boat into deeper water as fast as possible, but as far as we can tell the two men on shore are not in pursuit and do not seem to have called for reinforcements. It's just as well – our boat is not exactly the speediest of getaway craft.

I'm relieved. While family and friends at home are worried I'm going to be either caught in a Taliban ambush, shot by a crazed religious fanatic or stranded in the midst of a nuclear war, it looked for a few minutes as if I was going to be arrested for poaching ducks instead. As a former fish and game reporter I would never have lived it down.

Liaquat is recounting the tale of his hunt and shivering uncontrollably. I can hear his teeth chattering and I'm at the other end of the boat. I'd been dangling my feet in the water before he went swimming and thought it quite warm. But Liaquat has no surplus body fat and the long time he spent immobile while lining up his quarry has clearly taken its toll.

Mohammed, Nadeem and Inham are plucking and gutting the ducks. They're flinging feathers and guts into the river and because we are moving at the same speed as the current we travel for several kilometres surrounded by bobbing feet, beaks and innards. While we are still travelling in convoy with the duck remains Mohammed starts preparing lunch – by washing the vegetables in the river. He then rinses all our plates before serving up.

Javeed points far down stream to a grey structure on the

horizon. This is the Ghazi Ghat bridge and the place where we will leave the boat. It will take about two hours to get there because the main channel is snaking back and forth across the river bed. The rudder is making deep, shuddering groans as Liaquat manoeuvres us into the river's bends. It must be over 30°C, a perfect winter's day in the Punjab. Imran is combing his hair with a broken-toothed comb almost as long as his arm. Javeed, watched by his brothers, is making me a jet fighter from a cigarette packet.

When we can see the bridge clearly Mujahid begins scanning the bank for any sign of our jeep. We can't see it anywhere but as the sun begins to dip towards the bridge the dolphins, absent during the heat of the day, return. Indus dolphins don't leap clear of the water but these ones are arching high so we have our best views yet of the top side of their bodies. We moor near the mouth of a small stream, close enough to the bridge to hear the roar of the constant stream of trucks that is crossing it, and discover that this must be one of the dolphins' favourite fishing grounds. Three or four of them are swimming in large circles just beyond the boat. We watch them until the ever-present dust in the atmosphere turns the sun blood red and the lights of the trucks begin to blind us.

lahore is lahore

Progress through the congested bazaars inside Lahore's walled old city can be a slow business. The narrow winding lanes are often blocked by men pushing carts loaded with goods, everything from piles of towels to mounds of oranges. And it takes only one small group of veiled women to stop outside a fabric shop and everyone else comes to a grinding halt too.

There are 13 gates set into the walls that were built by Moghul emperor Akbar in the 16th century. The gates provide access to numerous bazaars and to two of Lahore's landmark buildings, its fort and the Badshahi Mosque. I had always assumed that motor vehicles were banned from squeezing through the entrances, but I was wrong, because I'm now in a jeep heading straight for the archway under the Delhi Gate.

Mujahid is determined to park the jeep inside the old city, despite the fact we are already in a gridlock of other vehicles that clearly haven't been able to find a park even in the streets immediately outside the walls. But, like men the world over, Mujahid is sure he can find the one parking space every other driver has overlooked. Getting through the gate itself is a challenge. It may have been designed to allow an elephant to pass under in the glory days of the Moghul empire, but nowadays enterprising hawkers have set up small stalls inside the deep archway and these, combined with the width of the jeep, mean there is no room for manoeuvre.

'Are you sure it wouldn't be easier to park outside and walk?' I suggest. Silly question – admitting defeat is not in Mujahid's nature.

'Did you say something?' he says, but I know he's heard me.

It's comforting that everyone is moving in the same direction as we are. I'm impressed – one-way traffic through a bazaar is a radical idea here. We are moving so slowly the jeep is on the verge of stalling so I have time to window-shop. Men are sitting on their haunches behind squares of brightly coloured cotton. On these are spread plastic combs in lurid colours, torches, padlocks and ballpoint pens.

We eventually emerge through the other side of the gate, but only after Mujahid leans out his window and gets one of the men to move his display out of the way. 'See?' he says, looking at me smugly. I point ahead. Two motorised rickshaws, side by side and filling the lane, are directly in front of us, about 2 metres from the jeep's front bumper. Clearly this is not one-way.

We gaze implacably at each other. The two rickshaw wallahs are hunched slightly over their handlebars and peer at us through windscreens almost totally obscured with multicoloured stickers and dangling tassels. Both have identical moustaches. It's like having double vision. As we sit there, neither side prepared to budge, donkey cart, handcart and pedestrian traffic begins to build up behind us like water in a dam. Every now and then a lone shopper squeezes past, banging their hands on the canvas of the jeep or the pressed metal decorations on the side of the rickshaw, in protest against our presence.

'There are three things I would remove from Lahore if I was in charge,' Mujahid says, regarding the scene with complete equanimity, 'donkeys, rickshaws and women, but maybe not in that order.'

Although I'm tempted to begin a discussion on Mujahid's attitude to women, the time doesn't seem quite right. I'm trying to quell a growing feeling of claustrophobia as the tide of Lahoris begins to deepen around us. A woman beggar reaches in the open passenger window and lays a scrawny hand on my arm. I try to move it and her fingers dig into my skin. I hate being clawed at like this and have to shake her off.

Eventually, after Mujahid and the rickshaw drivers exchange a graphic series of hand gestures, they give way. This involves evicting the passengers from one of the rickshaws and lifting it bodily into the tiniest of cul de sacs so we can squeeze past. It would have been easier for us to back through the gateway but I don't dare suggest it.

Mujahid plans to park in the courtyard outside the Wazir Khan mosque which is just a few metres away on our left, down another alleyway. At present the mosque is obscured by the crumbling buildings that line the bazaar, a dense cobweb of electricity wires and fluttering displays of dupattas and shawls. As we try to turn into this alleyway we encounter another motorist. To allow him out we have to overshoot the entrance.

Surely we'll give up now? But no, heedless of the throngs of people, the appearance of a man in a dhoti leading a camel with three small children perched on top and the arrival of another swarm of rickshaws, Mujahid begins to back the jeep into the alley leading to the mosque.

'You have to be joking,' I say.

'Just look out your side and tell me if I'm going to run over that beggar.'

Sure enough, less than a metre from the back wheel, sits an elderly woman, leaning against a wall, one leg outstretched. She is watching the jeep reverse towards her but either cannot or will not move.

Mujahid, meanwhile, is engaged in conversation with the clothing stall owner on his side. In fact the owner has to climb into his stall to avoid being flattened but he seems unconcerned and is suggesting we might like to buy a bolt of cloth while we are passing. You wouldn't even be able to slip a chapatti between the walls of the lane and the jeep. Centimetre by centimetre we reverse out of the bazaar traffic with the beggar playing a superb game of brinkmanship, not standing up until her foot is just about under the wheel. She then demands money for being disturbed, which Mujahid ignores.

We reverse into the Wazir Khan mosque car park, past a group of women who are making quilts on a raised concrete platform near the entranceway. 'Parking is becoming a real problem in this city,' Mujahid says.

Even our unconventional approach doesn't spoil the sight of this wonderfully ornamental mosque. The walls and minarets are covered with intricate mosaics in shades of yellow, orange, blue and green. Geometric designs frame stylised bouquets of flowers, their colours still vibrant after nearly 400 years. A flock of pigeons briefly takes to the air as we cross the courtyard in our bare feet as custom dictates.

We are not planning to linger here though, but to cross the old city to the Badshahi Mosque, one of the largest in the world. It is a landmark in Lahore, my favourite Pakistani city, the country's vibrant heart. There are the attractions of its architecture, history, culture, food and people but there is also something intangible. Even the Lahoris seem to struggle to define it and often fall back on an old but apt quotation, 'Lahore is Lahore'.

Our walk takes us deep into the bazaars. Mujahid hates even the suggestion of shopping, so I soon lose sight of him as I dawdle through the lanes.

My first stop is at a bangle shop, actually a stall about 1 metre wide and 2 metres deep. The shopkeeper can only get in and out by climbing over the front counter. Behind him and on both sides are floor to ceiling shelves of bangles that glitter and sparkle in the light from the naked bulbs.

Most of the bangles are glass in bright primary colours and some have been dipped in metallic glitters. They are usually sold by the dozen and you can mix and match colours and designs. I point out the ones I want to try and the shopkeeper holds my right hand, squeezing my thumb flat, and pushes a dozen red and gold bracelets over my fingers and up to my elbow. We add another set. They rattle together satisfyingly and tiny specks of glitter become stuck on the hairs on my arm.

A dozen bangles cost only a few dollars. I know they are fragile and won't last forever but even Pakistani women with much smaller disposable incomes than mine treat them as ephemeral possessions. When too many in the set have snapped it's simply an excuse to go back to the bazaar to buy some more.

Near my bracelet seller is a more upmarket jeweller who stocks wedding jewellery. His window display gleams with bright yellow gold bracelets, hair decorations, heart-shaped necklaces and, most exotic of all, nose rings with chains that loop across the cheek to an earring. Some of the pieces are set with rubies and pearls.

Further into the bazaar is a fabric shop specialising in wedding and special occasion shalwar kameez and saris. Seated inside, a mother and two daughters are watching a rather unusual one-man fashion show. A young moustached assistant is standing in front of them clad in a length of brilliant red sari material encrusted with gold embroidery. He even has the matching dupatta draped over his head and is peering coyly out from underneath it.

The well-upholstered shop owner invites me in. The women beckon as well, and make a space for me. Already piled up beside them are saris in peacock blue and ivory that they plan to buy. Together we watch as the shopkeeper unfurls some bolts of silk and waves of purple, maroon and emerald green ripple over the display platform. The colours and textures work on me like a drug – I'm intoxicated.

Mujahid appears in the doorway and rolls his eyes. 'I am waiting 15 minutes for you. What are you doing? Why are you looking at silk when you have no money to buy it? I don't understand women!'

The concept of New Age men may not be exactly making inroads in Pakistan but it is clear that men from the West and the East are equally mystified by women's shopping habits. I'm almost dragged out of the shop, having to first politely decline the invitation from Rosina and her mother to come to their house for dinner and the plea from the shopkeeper that I really do need a wedding sari to take home.

At an intersection I come across a blanket stall run by a family of black-bearded Afghan Pathans. Their shop is an explosion of vivid primary colours and fluorescents. In direct contrast the three men are dressed soberly in muted brown and grey shalwar kameez, topped with white embroidered skull caps. Wondering how Afghans, even ones living in Lahore, might react to a visit from a Westerner in these post-War on Terror days, I step into the shop to look at the blankets. Certainly business must always come first so I'm met with smiles and an invitation to sit, but there is no hint of animosity. I ask Mujahid to take a photo. 'Oh good, now everyone in New Zealand will think the bazaars are full of Taliban.'

Bazaars are often loosely arranged by product type: there are motor cycle sections, rows of shops devoted to stainless steel kitchenware, even an outdoor line-up of poster stalls. I've stumbled into cosmetics alley and am intrigued by all the jars and tubes of skin-whitening products. Pale skin is very desirable here and even many men will often go to some trouble to stop themselves tanning. When I was in the desert of Baluchistan all three of my Wakhi companions (who are naturally fair-skinned) borrowed sunblock from me. How strange that while women in Lahore are spending time and money trying to lighten their skin, in much of the world women are using ointments and lotions to give themselves a tan.

A row of skinned chickens dangling from hooks announces I have reached a food bazaar. I hurry past the butchers where the meat is sometimes swarming with flies, and pools of blood announce recent kills, but I linger at the other stalls. Vendors have gone to enormous trouble building pyramids of citrus fruits and apples, there are radishes lined up in orderly lines like missiles, icy green mountains of lettuces and chillies artistically arranged on cane trays. When I ask the price of the apples, the shopkeeper takes out a knife and cuts me a piece to try before I buy.

The dried fruit stalls are festooned with thick ropes of dried apricots hanging from the ceiling. Underneath these, stall-holders sit languidly waving feather dusters to keep the flies at bay. I'm given a handful of dried mulberries to eat. They look like desiccated raspberries but have a sharp strong flavour.

The most exotic sights are in the spice stalls where perfectly fashioned cones of powdered spices in every shade of gold, orange and brown have been built up painstakingly on metal plates. There are also hessian sacks of dried fennel, cardamom and cumin seeds, and some large seed heads that I have trouble identifying. That is until the storekeeper mimes having a smoke – they are opium poppies. He's asking me if I would prefer to buy some hashish instead when Mujahid returns again to drag me from the bazaar. 'First silk, now drugs – you cannot be left alone in here.'

He's told me this before. During a visit to the bazaar of Peshawar, I had also been guilty of dawdling. But this time it had more dramatic consequences. I was walking past an enticing array of brassware shops, paying more attention to their wares than to where I was going. So I was caught completely by surprise when one of a group of young men who were walking towards me, reached out and groped me. I let out a startled yelp, which Mujahid, who was several metres ahead, heard. He asked me what was wrong.

'One of those guys just grabbed my breast!'

'Which one?'

'What the hell does that matter? He shouldn't have done it to either of them!'

'I mean, which man,' Mujahid said patiently, his mouth twitching slightly. 'If you can recognise him I will go after him.'

I was relieved I couldn't tell him. The thought of a punch-up in a bazaar where almost everyone was armed did not seem worth the slight besmirching of my honour.

Back in the Lahore bazaar, two women in skin-tight animal print tights, gold lamé blouses and stiletto heels pass us. If I'd seen a polar bear stroll by I could not have been more stunned. I'm even more amazed when they turn around and I see their eyes have a thick outline of kohl or black eye-liner. 'They are not girls,' Mujahid explains, with a slight tinge of regret, 'they are transvestite dancers.' It's appropriate to see them near the fort. In the days of the Moghul empire a small door let into the fort walls was used by the emperors to make discreet visits to the dancing girls.

The Moghul empire dominated the Indian subcontinent for three centuries and rivalled its contemporary European empires. The first emperor (a descendant of the Mongolian conqueror Timur or Tamerlane) came to Lahore in 1524. But it was Akbar the Great in the 16th century, and especially his 17th-century descendants Jahangir and Shah Jahan, who were responsible for Lahore's Moghul treasures.

The Lahore fort was built by Akbar in 1566 and, although it served a military role right up to the time of the British, it was also a royal palace with special diwans or halls for public and private audiences with the emperor. Unlike the Moghul fort in Delhi, where you can be constantly plagued with touts and conmen, Lahore's fort is a peaceful oasis from the clamour of the bazaars and the modern city centre.

Scarlet bougainvillaea tumbles over the domed white roofs of small garden pavilions and there's a scent of jasmine and roses from the courtyards. There are few people here on a winter's afternoon so it's not difficult to stand alone and imagine the emperors swaggering past in their silken brocades, jewelled and enamelled daggers at their waistbands and necklaces of rubies, diamonds, emeralds and pearls around their necks.

The rulers and their wives revelled in luxury and beauty. In the Shish Mahal, the palace of mirrors built by Shah Jahan, almost every centimetre of the walls and ceiling is inlaid with tiny mirrors. An old man is sitting on the floor and after requesting a few rupees he lights a lamp and begins whirling it recklessly around above his head. We are surrounded in dancing light.

But the Shish Mahal is almost too flashy. My favourite building, which is nearby, was also built by Shah Jahan. A delicate marble pavilion with an ingeniously curved marble roof, it is called the Naulakha, which means nine lakhs (a lakh equals 100,000). No one seems sure whether this refers to the building costs or to the number of stones inlaid in the marble walls. This pietra dura work was also used in Shah Jahan's masterpiece, the Taj Mahal. It was the last of the great emperors, Aurangzeb, who built the Badshahi Mosque that lies across a courtyard from the fort. Its open courtyard can hold 60,000 worshippers but most times I'm there I share it with only a few dozen people.

Even when it is quiet, as it is today, there is always a handful of men in the prayer hall, sitting on the hand-woven carpets reading the Koran, or stretched out full length, asleep. Mosques are living places of worship. People come to pray or to read, take refuge from the sun or the rain, to chat, or simply to sit and absorb the atmosphere, as I do each time I come to Badshahi.

Two stonemasons are using mallets and chisels to reset some of the marble inlay in red sandstone panels they have taken down from the walls. It's good to see some restoration work under way here and in the fort. For too long some of these architectural gems have been left to quietly deteriorate with pollution, graffiti artists and even souvenir hunters taking their toll.

Propped up in another archway is a young man reading from the Koran and letting a string of prayer beads slip rhythmically through his fingers. Two small girls, who have left their parents in their wake, are running across the central courtyard. In their lemon and pink party dresses they look like little meringues. I'm watching them chasing pigeons when I hear a shout from near the mosque gateway: 'Don't you dare stand in that puddle.'

The broad Birmingham accent has me turning around to see who else has been ignoring the travel advisories. But there are no tourists there. The only other family in sight is a man accompanied by two young women in chiffon shalwar kameez and high heels. One of the women is trying to restrain a young boy in a *Star Wars* T-shirt who is intent on leaping in the pools of water near the central pool. As they draw closer to my archway, though, I hear the Brummie accent again. We smile and they come over to talk. They are Pakistanis from England who are in Lahore on holiday. 'I'd forgotten how dusty it is, and how polluted,' one of the women tells me.

It *is* grimy. Every time I return from the bazaar I'm astonished by how grubby my hands are and how my face feels as if it hasn't been washed for a month. And the diesel fumes from the rickshaws can be choking. But Lahore gets away with this, especially on a winter's night when the fountains in the traffic islands are playing and the flower shops are lit up, displaying their banks of multicoloured roses and enough gladioli spikes to make Dame Edna's day.

Because Pakistan is officially 'dry' it can be natural to assume there is no nightlife. I've learnt otherwise. One passion I share with many Lahoris out for a night on the town is going to the movies. It's not the blockbuster Western films I go to but Indian and Pakistani ones, the products of either the world's most prolific film studios, Bollywood (based in Mumbai or Bombay in India), or the smaller studios in Lahore, inevitably called Lollywood. Pakistan produces about 60 films a year. Production is a round-the-clock business and there is a fervent band of film fans who follow the latest gossip about the stars just as avidly as Hollywood antics are followed in the West.

The first film I went to in Lahore was screening at the Prince Cinema near the Lakshami Chowk (market). I went with a group of tourist guides, all men. We stepped out of the car into a lurid world of gigantic movie posters that were emblazoned on the theatre and surrounding walls, dwarfing the patrons below. Pictured on them were women with sultry, dark eyes wearing diaphanous saris and men with bristling arrogant moustaches armed to the teeth with a range of deadly automatic weapons. I had the feeling this was not going to be a night of subtle storylines.

There was an armed security guard on the door who ran a metal detector over all of us and enquired about the contents of my handbag. It was all a touch different to going to the movies at home where you could probably take an anti-aircraft gun into the theatre and no one would notice.

The entire foyer area appeared to be lined with tin and was painted bright green, as was the private box we were sitting in. Now I knew how the Queen must feel when she went to the theatre. I suspected my escorts would normally have sat in the cinema proper but obviously it was decided that a box was the appropriate place When Out with a Woman. Few of my companions had ever been to the movies with a female. Most had wives in the mountains who never came to the city.

We distributed ourselves among three tip-up bench seats. There was an art to managing these. If one person got up suddenly the others in the row would find they inadvertently bobbed up as well. This was something the Queen probably did not experience in her nights at the theatre.

The movie, *Mehndi Walay Hath* (Hands Painted in Henna), was already under way. I don't know how we'd managed to miss the start because we'd spent half an hour having cups of tea down the road while waiting for the theatre to open. But no one seemed to mind; in fact people continued to arrive and leave throughout the evening.

The screen was huge, the volume deafening. *Mehndi Walay Hath* was a Punjabi film, which meant I had to have whispered explanations of the plot from time to time. Not that anyone seemed to worry about the interruptions. People whistled loudly when the heroine was on screen, hissed at the bad guys and from time to time added the odd quip to the dialogue, sometimes getting a murmur of appreciation from the rest of the audience.

The heroine was played by Saima, one of Pakistan's most successful and highly paid actresses. With huge brown eyes, lips that could pout for Pakistan and a voluptuous figure, it was easy to see why almost the entire audience (I appeared to be the only female there) was transfixed when she was on screen.

The plot was a simple one, at least in a Pakistani context. Young beautiful girl of rich land-owning parents is approaching marriageable age. But because of an unfortunate legal glitch her family decide she cannot marry because if she does half the family fortune will vanish. The solution is to marry her to the Koran, which will entail a life of chastity and rather a lot of reading. Alas, our heroine has fallen in love with one of her father's workers, played by a Pakistani pin-up boy, Momi Rana.

After his first appearance my friends, temporarily ignoring the action on the screen, asked me what I thought of him. I told them I gave him a 9.5 out of 10.

'Only 9.5?' someone said.

I pointed out that there's always room for improvement, but they found that hard to believe. This was a Pakistani man, after all. How could I not give him a 10?

When Momi found out about the 'wedding' he decided he must take his broken heart and leave the farm forever. But before he did the couple cavorted knee-deep in a field full of mustard flowers. The audience went wild. As he left home there was a perfect excuse for one of the singing and dancing extravaganzas that make the subcontinent's films unique. A recently harvested field heaved with gyrating women with jiggling bosoms and there were lingering shots of Momi singing and looking alluringly at the screen through his long lashes. Despite the fact that all the women were in traditional garb, there was no shortage of female charms on display – a triumph of cinematographic ingenuity over censorship.

The music was romping along and booming off the metal walls. The audience weren't quite bopping in the aisle but they were close. We were all having a great time. An intermission sign popped up after an hour and we headed outside to the stalls in the cinema. They sold fizzy drink (which had to be drunk on the spot so we could hand back the glass bottles), cigarettes and pan (the betel nut mixture popped in the mouth, chewed and later spat out).

The tone of the film changed abruptly in part two. Saima was now married to the Koran and, clearly not thinking much of her wedding night, was in floods of tears for days. Eventually Momi abducted her. The family set off to avenge this loss of honour. Four-wheel drives bristling with men armed with machine-guns and what appeared to be rocket launchers bounced their way to the love nest.

A bloody and protracted gunfight followed in which just about everyone died. There was so much death and destruction it was hard to take it very seriously. Every time a baddy met a sticky end the audience cheered and were equally stricken when one of the goodies was wiped out. And, despite the carnage, Saima retained her serenity and devastating good looks to the last frame. 'Punjabi films always end like that,' I was told. 'Next time we'll go to an Urdu one.'

And I have, and I love them all, and the atmosphere of the old-fashioned theatres where vendors bring ice creams and drinks to your seat even during the movie (and expect to be paid on the spot, which can be tricky in the dark). The films are not sophisticated, slick or pretentious but there is something refreshing about the lack of sex scenes and offensive language. The dance scenes are pure fun and the audience participation is infectious.

Near the movie theatres is another of Lahore's unique night-time attractions: a pedestrianised 'food street' developed to cater for Lahoris' well known love of eating. On my last visit, after Mujahid and I go to see an Urdu film that inexplicably features a bull-fighting scene in Spain, we make a tour of the stalls.

Each restaurant is open to the street and many of the chefs are cooking their specialities right beside the tables. Waiters tout for business, trying to entice the throngs of prospective diners walking down the centre of the street. Cooks sweat it out behind rotisseries crammed with kebabs, and assistants keep the charcoals glowing under the Baluchi sajji – the legs of mutton and whole chickens impaled on skewers and set upright in the coals. There are displays of unfamiliar looking glistening white and pink mounds. They turn out to be raw sheep and goat testicles.

We finally succumb to the pleas of a young waiter to choose his restaurant and order a Lahori speciality of fish cooked in a tandoor oven, served with cornbread and spinach. The fish is melt-in-the-mouth and delicately spiced, and the corn bread has a slightly crunchy crust. A curry arrives next. I ask what meat is in it.

'Just try it first,' Mujahid says.

After checking there are no obscure body parts floating in it, I do so. It has a rich but unidentifiable taste.

'It's camel meat,' Mujahid says.

I try not to think about the camel that carried me, even if at times it had not exactly been without complaint, through the Baluchistan Desert.

Many of the people strolling down Food Street are eating from tiny terracotta dishes that fit into the palms of their hands. The dishes come with lids that have to be broken off, revealing keer, a local version of rice pudding.

Also on the menu for dessert are jelabees, bright orange squiggles of deep-fried pastry soaked in sugar syrup. I buy one for old time's sake. The first time I'd ever tried one was at Murree Christian School. The cooks used to make them as a treat for afternoon tea. Trays piled with sticky jelabees would be carried onto the grassed terrace behind the dining room. Kids and staff would demolish them in seconds. I've associated them ever since with a view of the distant Karakorams framed by deodar pines.

Our final stop in Food Street is to buy Kashmiri tea from an elderly man with a creased face and straggling white beard. He is sitting cross-legged on a platform, in front of him a shallow round pan nearly a metre across. The tea, a frothy mixture the colour of milk chocolate, is bubbling inside it. Kashmiri tea is made from green (unfermented) tea leaves. Milk or cream, sugar and cardamom is added and the mix is boiled. The final touch is a sprinkling of nuts such as almonds or pistachio over the top.

I drink it slowly, aware this is my last bazaar on this trip. The Lahore night is warm, and a kaleidoscope of people pass by. Mujahid is sighing over the beauty of Lahori women and I can see why. They are wearing designer shalwar kameez that shimmer with metallic threads, their heads are uncovered revealing jet black hair gleaming in the street lights. They walk tall, confident of the effect they are having on the watching diners and of their growing influence in society.

They are Pakistan's middle class, often well-educated, liberal women who are forging their own path through the complexities of Islamic and cultural traditions. They don't want Western feminists telling them to shed their shalwar kameez or how to transform their husbands into New Age men. Pakistan is full of strong women who are already making their mark with human rights issues, sometimes even in the face of death threats from ultra-conservatives.

A group of three girls in their early 20s sweeps past, arm in arm, and all cheekily flash alluring smiles at Mujahid.

'You stay where you are and drink your chai,' I tell him.

'Why did Allah send me a bossy Kiwi journalist to work with?'

I tell him it's good for his imperilled soul and that I'd like another cup of Kashmiri tea.

On the way home we drive past illuminated billboards for KFC and McDonald's which are advertising Ramazan specials. Not even the dawn to dusk fasting prevents these multinational juggernauts from doing good business. They just rearrange their opening hours and cater for the brisk after-dark trade.

Back at the Lahore apartment that is home to an extended family of Wakhi men who work in the city, I climb the stairs to the flat roof. I should be packing because I'm going home the next day but I'm trying to put it off. From up here I can see the illuminated gold sickle on top of the nearest mosque. Just along from it are the golden arches of a McDonald's restaurant.

Dupattas hanging on a clothesline on the neighbouring roof-top waft gently in the breeze, as does the aroma of frying pakoras. There is a slight whiff of drain from the alleyway below and a mangy dog is nosing among a pile of rubbish that has been swept into a corner of the street. It will probably never be shifted but will be slowly redistributed around the alley.

The repellent and the exotic are the two sides of the same coin. I've learnt to accept that; and to be neither blind to the country's faults nor to let them overwhelm me. I try to leave Western assumptions and misconceptions behind on the plane and over the years there is less mental excess baggage to bring home but a greater sense of loss.

Before I fly home I ask Mujahid to take me out to the Wagah border that is the only open land crossing between Pakistan and India. We take with us a friend of Mujahid's (yet another Wakhi called Karim) and a little boy with enormous eyes whose nickname is Chota (Little) Shahjee. He is the son of Shahjee, one of my companions in the desert. Each morning and night at the border the two countries indulge in a piece of jingoistic open-air theatre as they open and close the border gates. I want to see what impact recent tensions might have had on the ceremony.

A few kilometres from the border is a ridge of earthworks that is presumably some kind of recently constructed tank trap, but otherwise life is carrying on completely as normal on this side of the world's most volatile border. Scruffy children are herding the family buffaloes home, a milk seller with two bulbous brass pots on each side of his bike is wobbling along the road and the roadside bazaars are bursting with winter vegetables. Towels with grubby head-shaped patches in their centres are drying on lines above the barber shops.

'I thought everyone had moved out of the border area?'

'You watch too much television,' Mujahid says, swerving the jeep around an overloaded Suzuki minivan that has pulled out in front of us. 'These drivers are so bloody bad.'

It takes only about 45 minutes to drive from the apartment to the border and by the time we reach it Chota Shahjee is fast asleep in Karim's lap. We revive him sufficiently so he can walk with us from the car park to the border proper.

Since I was here last the Pakistanis and Indians have engaged in some major building work. It now looks like a rather elongated cricket stadium. On 'our' side is a new red brick semi-circular grandstand with offices on the ground floor for the Pakistan Rangers (the military unit dedicated to border patrol). This was built in response to the Indians' construction of an even larger tiered seating area. The crowds which flock to the ceremonies each day now have a much better view of each other. Fervent displays of patriotism are more satisfying if the other side can see them.

As we walk under the archway that pierces the centre of the grandstand and head for a front row seat just a few metres from the gate, I'm struck again how much this is like the military answer to a subcontinental one-day cricket clash. Pakistani pop music blares from loudspeakers and adds a festive touch to the atmosphere. Tall brick pillars emblazoned with the Pakistani star and moon flank the gate and behind them are two flagpoles. One flies the green and white Pakistani flag, the other India's orange, white and green-striped one. Beyond the flags is India's metal barrier.

Several members of the Pakistani Rangers are standing near

the gate making last-minute adjustments to their uniforms. The grey material of their shalwar kameez has been woven with metallic thread so it catches the light. Their black turbans have a stiff veil that fans out behind the head and down the back. Red cummerbunds and neckerchiefs provide a splash of colour and their black shoes are soled with metal plates that click on the tarmac.

A member of the Pakistani audience comes running down the centre of the road holding an outsize Pakistani flag. He waves it energetically in front of us, and then standing directly in front of the open gate, lifts the flag high in the direction of the opposition grandstand. An Indian immediately stands up and begins waving his flag in defiance. There are cheers from both sides and a chant of 'Allah akbar' from the Pakistanis. The Indians reply but it is impossible to pick out the words.

A newspaper seller walks past and approaches one of the guards near the gate. The guard takes the stack of papers and wanders across the border where he hands the newspapers to his Indian offsider who gives him a pile in return. They chat, then carry the papers away, presumably to their respective mess rooms where they'll be able to read about border tensions. A sound of running water behind us alerts us that the ceremony is about to start. There's an artificial waterfall in the corner of the parade ground which is always switched on just beforehand. A border guard heads directly for me and politely points to the women's side of the road. I cross over and am immediately adopted by four teenage girls who have come with their Pakistani army officer father to see the ceremony.

From the grandstand end of the Pakistani stretch of the pitch, two soldiers appear side by side goose-stepping at double-quick time towards the border. A rising tide of clapping and cheering accompanies them as if they were batsmen walking out to open the innings. Meanwhile in India two guards in khaki trousers and red puttees are charging in from their end like fast bowlers, accompanied by the vocal encouragement of their supporters. It's gloriously Gilbert and Sullivan and shamelessly nationalistic. I should hate all this sabre-rattling. But I can't help but be swept along with the Pakistanis' fervour. I love these people.

I hate the pollution and the squalor that the homeless are forced to live in. It angers me to see schools with no teachers and villages with no medical clinics, when the government funds armed forces with more than half a million personnel and a multimillion-dollar nuclear weapons programme. And it's distressing to hear about ignorant village mullahs (religious leaders) encouraging the repression of women. But that's not the full picture, although it is the one that is purveyed in the West. And it does Pakistan a grave disservice.

I admire the Pakistanis' irrepressible belief that one day their opinions will count, despite spending more years since their independence in 1947 under dictators than democratically elected governments; I can empathise with their nation thumbing its nose at world powers that want to tell them how to run their country; and I pray with them that one day their politicians will allow them to realise their full potential.

Two of the soldiers take up their positions beside the flagpoles. We stand to sing the national anthem. My companions encourage me to sing along. When we finish, the soldiers manning the ropes begin to unwind them at a furious pace. The Pakistani is first to unravel all of his.

'That is good, we won,' says the girl beside me. 'You must clap more. But it is a bit silly,' she adds, as an afterthought.

We now undertake a rousing chant of 'Pakistan zindabad'. The girls are smiling at me encouragingly as I join in. Across the road Mujahid and Karim are grinning. Several of the girls reach out for my arm to make sure I turn around to look back at the grandstand. A lone Pakistani solider is standing there. He tosses his head like a stallion in the starting gates and then sets off towards the gate at a tremendous pace, goose-stepping so high his foot almost appears to strike his forehead.

The crowd goes wild. Just before the border he stops. Then, with a great clatter of shoe plates, he makes a stomping half-turn and finishes, glowering over one shoulder at his counterpart on the other side of the border. The only movement is the twitching of his moustache. We engulf him in an enthusiastic cheer of 'Allah akbar'.

'Do you think he is handsome?' one of the girls asks.

'Yes, very.'

'So, you like our country?'

'I love Pakistan, it is my second home.'

They huddle together and whisper. 'We would like you to come to our house for tea and bring your son.'

My son?

'Your little boy over there with your husband,' the girl closest to me says, pointing at Chota Shahjee who is sitting on Karim's shoulders.

'No, no, that's not my husband.'

'We are sorry. Then the other man is your husband.'

I explain that none of the trio in the men's section is related to me in any way.

But there's no time for me to sort out the confusion because the ceremony is drawing to its conclusion. A tall Pathan soldier, his uniform glinting in the sun, steps up to the open gate and gives it a tremendous heave. It shoots across the road, closing with a clang.

glossary

burqa – head to foot covering worn by some Muslim women. Some burqas have an opening for the eyes, others have a crocheted panel.

chai – tea (usually black tea boiled up with the milk and sugar).

chapatti – a wholemeal unleavened bread cooked on a flat metal plate.

charpoi – a wooden-framed bed with a base of woven and knotted rope.

chowkidar – caretaker.

chunnah – savoury crunchy snacks (the Pakistani equivalent of potato crisps).

dacoits – robbers or bandits.

dhal – lentil curry.

dhoti – a long loincloth worn by men. Not common in Pakistan but sometimes seen in more southern areas.

dudh wallah – milk seller.

dupatta – a long wide scarf always worn by women dressed in shalwar kameez. It is usually draped across the bust and/or over the head.

Inshallah – if Allah wills it.

Islam – the religion of the Muslims who believe that there is one God (Allah) and that Mohammed is his Prophet. Islam means submission to Allah.

Kalashnikov – Russian assault rifle (those found in Pakistan are likely to be copies made locally).

Koran – the sacred book of Muslims containing the word of Allah as revealed to his prophet Mohammed.

Masha Allah – thanks to Allah.

memsahib – a term of respect, from the days of the Raj, for a European married woman.

missahib – as above, but for an unmarried woman.

Moghul – the Muslim dynasty founded in 1526 that ruled the Indian subcontinent for more than 300 years.

mosque – the Muslim place of worship.

muezzin – the person who calls Muslims to prayer (although sometimes nowadays it is a recorded voice broadcast from the minarets).

mujahideen – Muslims who engage in jihad or a holy struggle. Many Muslims interpret jihad as an inner spiritual struggle but in the West it is usually (wrongly) interpreted as meaning holy war.

Muslims – followers of Islam.

naan – yeast bread, cooked in large rounds in a tandoor (oven).

pakora – deep-fried spoonful of vegetables in a lentil flour batter.